CHRISTIAN HÜMBS

▼

BAKE
TO
IMPRESS

CHRISTIAN HÜMBS

▼

BAKE
TO
IMPRESS

WITH PHOTOGRAPHY BY
JAN C. BRETTSCHNEIDER

▼

CONTENTS

100 show-stopping cakes & desserts

FOREWORD
Page 7

INTRODUCTION
Page 9

QUICK & EASY
Page 12

INTERNATIONAL CLASSICS
Page 78

SPECIAL & UNUSUAL
Page 140

MASTER BAKING TO IMPRESS
Page 190

**BASIC RECIPES · SOURCES · ACKNOWLEDGEMENTS
BAKING NOTES · INDEX**
Page 216

▼

WRITING A BAKING BOOK

is no easy task

I honestly thought it would be easier! But no. First you have to choose between the competing recipes tumbling about in your head, then you have to consider what information you need to give so that the reader has as much knowledge as possible at their fingertips and – when you're finally done – you need to be able to live with the fact that your recipes will now be immortalized in print with little chance of changing anything ever again!

Despite all this, I was instantly keen to write a book which could truly convey the enormous diversity of pâtisseries and baked goods, a book to give people a real foundation in baking know-how. And how amazing to get the opportunity to be involved in such a project.

I have always sought outlets to express myself creatively. At one time I studied painting and originally I wanted to be a stucco artist. When I had to change jobs for health reasons and a career in gastronomy was suggested to me, I opted for pâtisserie training, quite simply because of the far more humane working hours in contrast to the punishing life of a chef. I quickly sensed that this was truly the right path for me, but I also noticed that in this profession I was somewhat limited in terms of creative outlets. So I undertook a chef's training as well. That was the real breakthrough! For me, the combination of cooking and baking turned out to be an absolute passion. Now, I can't imagine finding such complete creative expression in any other field.

Even today it never ceases to give me pleasure, seeing the multitude of products (chocolate, fruit, vegetables) you can use to bring the most outrageous creations to the table. I've been working in this trade for 16 years now and not a single day has been boring. It gives me a real kick to constantly broaden my horizons and benefit from new technologies and other developments. For me, pâtisserie is like a tree: the trunk is formed of the core baking skills central to the discipline; extending out from that are decorative icing, sugar craft and the art of the chocolatier or – at the very highest level – the master pâtissier. However, all these branches have one thing in common with domestic baking in your own kitchen: the heart and soul that you put into your work. The pride you feel when you get the hang of a super-tricky chocolate ganache at the very first attempt; or indeed the fury when your home-made puff pastry is a complete flop. Quite simply, it's all about the fun to be had in your kitchen, producing sweet masterpieces with your own hands. It might sound a bit corny, but you just don't get that with a bought cake or pre-packaged pudding.

I will feel that I have succeeded with this book if it encourages you to conjure up a home-made cake that puts a smile on the faces of your guests and really gets their taste buds rejoicing. So let yourself be inspired by the following pages.

Yours, Christian Hümbs

▼

BAKE TO IMPRESS

Cakes, Tarts, Cupcakes & Co.

My aim with this book is to show you just how much fun it is to get stuck into baking the most delicious cakes, tarts, cupcakes, cookies, and brownies at home. No doubt some of you already have several years baking experience and a fail-safe repertoire under your belt. Others may need more detailed instructions before they can get going. I want to share my professional expertise with all of you. So I have developed these 100 recipes for all levels. In these pages you will find an array of sweet classics – such as creamy tiramisu, New York-style cheesecake, or marshmallows – which will always have a place in my kitchen and with which I have no desire to tinker. At the other end of the scale, you will find innovative, unfamiliar flavour combinations such as green tea, white chocolate and macadamia brownies, or even cronuts with yuzu jelly and vanilla cream filling. I hope these will expand your horizons in totally new ways.

Some of the recipes are really easy to follow even for novice bakers; others might push you to your limits or beyond. But that is the wonderful thing: there is something for everyone here! Today you might fancy a really simple apple cake; tomorrow maybe you'll be tempted by the more challenging macarons, the so-called royalty of classic French pâtisserie. Whatever you choose, you should stick to some basic principles to achieve the best possible results. The most important of these principles (and, therefore, the foundation for success) concerns the raw ingredients you use. You will never be able to prepare a mind-blowing chocolate mousse using the cheapest chocolate or poor-quality flavourings.

This doesn't necessarily mean your kitchen has to be stocked with hazelnuts from Piedmont or Sicilian pistachios, but anyone hoping for a Ferrari driving experience is never going to be happy with a second-hand small car. In other words: choose your ingredients carefully if you want good results. You don't always need to buy absolutely top-class goods – their cost is usually a big deterrent – but there are lots of excellent, high-quality ingredients that won't break the bank and will still ensure the most fantastic results.

Another important consideration is to pay attention to which produce is in season and adjust your baking to accommodate this. If you are trying to rustle up delicious aromatic fruit to make a cherry cake in December, you are on a hiding to nothing. Instead, when rhubarb is sprouting at the start of spring, why not have a go at making a crisp rhubarb tart topped with meringue? It's not just that the ingredients have a quite different flavour when they are properly ripe, it's also definitely cheaper than going out in winter to buy pallid strawberries air-freighted in from Israel. Besides, nowadays there is also really good-quality frozen produce available. You just need to decide what you are going to be using the frozen fruit for: cooking up jam or making a topping, no problem; as decoration on your dessert, no way. The best tip I can give you in this regard is to really keep your eyes open and observe what is going on in the garden or – if you don't have one – on local market stalls. These can often be the best source of seasonal baking inspiration.

Before you get started, there is one more thing to bear in mind: baking takes time! Always schedule in enough time to achieve good results. If you rush things, you can hardly be surprised when your cake ends up stodgy or its icing doesn't set properly. Some processes – such as proving bread dough or cooling down a cream – simply can't be hurried, or at least not without damaging the outcome. Give yourself time to read a recipe through once or twice before you start, so you don't forget any of the steps or overlook any ingredient or utensil required. The preparation is just as important as the baking itself. Nothing is more annoying than finding out halfway through the job that the sugar has run out or you don't have the right baking tin in your cupboard. If possible, gather the equipment you need to hand, weigh out the ingredients, and have everything else the recipe requires ready in advance.

If you are a baking novice, try to keep as closely as possible to the recipe. Later, when you've gained a little experience, you may be able to play around a bit with one or other of the ingredients. Perhaps the lavender tart you are making for your guests would taste even better with twice the amount of fresh lavender flowers? Try it!

If you follow all these basic principles you will be off to a secure start. Also, you will find within the recipes that I provide the odd tip which will turn you into a true star baker. If that's still not enough for you, and you want to develop novel creations that are completely your own, the following information will definitely help you to discover original and first-rate flavour combinations.

The number one product in baking and pâtisserie is chocolate. No other ingredient can be combined in quite so many different ways as this raw material. It is a fabulous partner for a range of other produce, from citrus fruits (or fruits in general), to various teas, and even vegetables. However, be aware of chocolate's dark side as well.

Although cocoa powder is wonderful for emphasizing certain flavours, it also readily dominates the palate and has a very powerful presence in the mouth (the same applies to matcha tea, by the way). Even small quantities can end up being overly strong and leave little room for other flavour notes and aromas.

Citrus fruits in whatever form – be it in lemon curd or as a jelly for a tart filling – can be used to reduce the heaviness of sweet, doughy pastries and make them taste lighter. Along with acidic complements from the dairy family (such as crème fraîche or soured cream), citrus fruits can lend a fresh note to your desserts. And in addition to regular lemons and limes you could try out the up-and-coming but still rather less well-known Asian citrus fruit yuzu, which has floral notes as well as aromatic freshness. It beautifully flatters the sweetness of white chocolate, for example, while also balancing out the flavours really well; what you might call a perfect match.

Ultimately it all comes down to experience when you are finding out for yourself which products and flavours go well together. So the name of the game is: taste, taste, taste! And just accept that to start with you might occasionally produce something that has to be binned… but don't let that discourage you from trying something out of the ordinary every so often. In my work as a pâtissier, for example, it is a great passion of mine to create outlandish, innovative desserts with vegetables. Although this isn't quite as applicable in the domestic kitchen, it is still a useful principle for the home baker to know that fresh vegetables always lend moistness to baked goods. Maybe you are already familiar with the carrots in carrot cake, but why not take some pumpkin, fennel or beetroot which have been finely grated, or cooked and puréed, and stir them into your batter or dough to give your cake or bread more moisture? The higher the proportion of vegetables, the more luscious the baked result will be.

If you want to forge new paths in terms of flavours, the best place to start is with more traditional taste combinations for pâtisserie, such as sweet-and-sour. In this book I've achieved this, for instance, in a cherry tart with balsamic vinegar, where sweet cherries are combined with acidic vinegar and a bitter chocolate coating. For the chocolate you could experiment with single-origin varieties that have their own strong personalities, or with different cocoa solids percentages. Another particularly delicious marriage is that of beetroot and white chocolate; the intense sweetness of the chocolate works superbly with the bitter earthiness of the red tuber. Over time you will discover the combinations that are most delicious for you.

Baking is such a broad subject that there is scope for everyone to discover their own favourite branch. Just always remain curious, have fun wielding your balloon whisk and piping bag, and enjoy astounding people with your creations.

▼

QUICK & EASY

Speedy success

....

If you want to surprise a friend
with a home-made cake at a moment's
notice, the super-fast goodies
on the next few pages are sure-fire
sensations. They look fantastic
and, most importantly, they
are utterly delicious.

▼

RASPBERRY CUPCAKES

with buttermilk

For the cakes: 75g (2½oz) unsalted butter, at room temperature, plus extra for the moulds (optional) • 175g (6oz) buttermilk • 250g (9oz) raspberries, fresh or thawed from frozen • 60g (2oz) caster sugar • seeds from ½ vanilla pod • pinch of salt • 2 small eggs • 200g (7oz) plain flour • 1½ tsp baking powder
For the topping: 300g (10oz) double cream • seeds from 1 vanilla pod • 75g (2½oz) icing sugar • 250g (9oz) fresh raspberries
Equipment: 12-hole muffin tray • 12 paper muffin cases (optional) • small piping bag with star nozzle

Makes 12   Prep: 20 mins + cooling   Baking time: 30–35 mins

1. Preheat the oven to 180°C (350°F/Gas 4). Butter the muffin moulds, or insert a paper case into each.

2. For the cake, use a hand-held blender to purée the buttermilk with 175g (6oz) of the raspberries in a high-sided beaker. Cream the butter in a bowl with half the sugar, the vanilla seeds, and salt, using an electric hand whisk. Separate the eggs. Add the egg yolks one at a time to the butter mix and whisk until well combined. Whisk in the raspberry purée.

3. Mix the flour with the baking powder and stir into the mix just enough for all the ingredients to be well combined. Use the scrupulously cleaned electric hand whisk to beat the egg whites in a bowl until stiff, gradually adding the remaining sugar and whisking to combine after every addition. Carefully fold them into the batter, one-third at a time.

4. Spoon the batter into the muffin tray moulds or cases. Divide the remaining raspberries over the cakes and press in lightly. Bake on the middle shelf of the preheated oven for 30–35 minutes until golden brown. Do not open the oven door during this time. Remove from the oven and let them rest in the tin for around 5 minutes. Then lift out the cupcakes and leave them to cool on a wire rack.

5. For the topping, beat the cream with the vanilla seeds and icing sugar, put this into a small piping bag fitted with a star nozzle, pipe onto the cakes and arrange the fresh raspberries on top.

▼

COCONUT BANANA MUFFINS

with white chocolate

For the cakes: 75g (2½oz) unsalted butter, at room temperature, plus extra for the moulds (optional) • 1 large banana, about 200g (7oz) • 175ml (6fl oz) coconut milk • 100g (3½oz) desiccated coconut, plus extra to garnish • 200g (7oz) plain flour • 1½ tsp baking powder • pinch of salt • 2 eggs • 60g (2oz) caster sugar • seeds from ½ vanilla pod
For the topping: white chocolate, coarsely grated • Caramel Sauce, to serve (optional, see p43)
Equipment: 12-hole muffin tray • 12 paper muffin cases (optional)

Makes 12   Prep: 20 mins + cooling   Baking time: 25 mins

1. Preheat the oven to 180°C (350°F/Gas 4). Butter the muffin moulds, or insert a paper case into each.

2. Peel the banana. Use a hand-held blender to purée it with the coconut milk in a high-sided beaker. Toast the desiccated coconut, including that for garnish, in a dry pan until golden brown. Leave to cool. Mix the flour, baking powder, salt, and 100g (3½oz) of the toasted coconut. Separate the eggs.

3. Use an electric hand whisk to cream the butter with half the sugar and the vanilla seeds in a bowl until light and fluffy. Gradually add the egg yolks and beat them into the butter and sugar mixture.

4. Use a wooden spoon to stir the banana purée and flour mix into the butter mix, stirring just enough to combine. Use the scrupulously cleaned electric hand whisk to beat the egg whites in a bowl until stiff, gradually adding the remaining sugar and whisking to combine after every addition. Carefully fold them into the batter, one-third at a time.

5. Spoon the batter into the muffin tray moulds or cases. Bake the muffins on the middle shelf of the preheated oven for around 25 minutes until golden brown. Do not open the oven door during this time. Remove from the oven and let them rest in the tin for around 5 minutes. Then lift out the muffins and leave them to cool on a wire rack. Sprinkle the muffins with the remaining toasted coconut and with the grated white chocolate and serve with caramel sauce (if using).

Tip: alternative mango and coconut muffins
You can make mango and coconut muffins in the same way. Just replace the banana with around 150g (5½oz) perfectly ripe mango. Really ripe mangoes smell wonderfully aromatic and the flesh of the fruit yields slightly when lightly pressed; remember this when shopping!

▼

PEANUT BUTTER APPLE MUFFINS

with caramel sauce

For the cakes: 3 tbsp flavourless vegetable oil, plus extra for the moulds (optional) • 2 apples, about 210g (7½oz) in total • 85g (3oz) dried apple rings • 190g (6¾oz) caster sugar • 2 eggs • 85g (3oz) smooth peanut butter, plus 5 tbsp extra for the topping • 210g (7½oz) plain flour • 2 tsp baking powder • 3½ tbsp milk • Caramel Sauce, to serve (see p43) • unsalted peanuts, roughly chopped, to serve
Equipment: 12-hole muffin tray • 12 paper muffin cases (optional) • small piping bag with star nozzle

Makes 12 Prep: 40 mins + cooling Baking time: 30 mins

1. Preheat the oven to 180°C (350°F/Gas 4). Oil the muffin moulds, or insert a paper case into each.

2. Peel the apples and finely grate the fruit, discarding the core. Finely chop the dried apple.

3. Use a hand-held blender to beat the sugar with the eggs in a high-sided beaker until light and fluffy. Gradually pour in the oil in a thin stream, mixing all the time, until you have a cream with the consistency of mayonnaise. Pour into a wider bowl.

4. Stir the peanut butter into the egg mixture and fold in the grated apple. Combine the flour with the baking powder and add to the mixture, alternating with the milk, and stirring just enough for all the ingredients to combine to a smooth consistency. Finally, fold in the dried apple.

5. Spoon the batter into the muffin tray moulds or cases. Bake the muffins on the middle shelf of the preheated oven for around 30 minutes until golden brown. Do not open the oven door during this time. Remove from the oven and let them rest in the tin for around another 5 minutes. Then lift out the muffins and leave them to cool on a wire rack.

6. Gently heat the peanut butter for the topping in a small saucepan, spoon it into a small piping bag fitted with a star nozzle and use to decorate the muffins. Drizzle the caramel sauce over the muffins and sprinkle with the peanuts.

▼

SPELT AND CHERRY MUFFINS

with acacia honey

For the cakes: 280ml (9½fl oz) flavourless vegetable oil, plus extra for the moulds (optional) • 220g (scant 8oz) wholemeal spelt flour • 30g (1oz) cocoa powder, plus extra for dusting (optional) • 3 tsp baking powder • 4 large eggs • 250g (9oz) acacia honey • 100g (3½oz) cherry purée (with about 10% sugar, see p219) • 20g (¾oz) icing sugar, plus extra for dusting (optional) • 1 tbsp cherry juice • about 150g (5½oz) cherries, pitted fresh, or from a jar
Equipment. 12-hole muffin tray • 12 paper muffin cases (optional)

Makes 12   Prep: 15 mins + cooling   Baking time: 30 mins

I love baking with spelt flour because of its versatility and delicate, malty flavour. In this recipe it provides a great partner for the cherries because together they give a fabulous marzipan-like flavour. The floral acacia honey complements those flavours beautifully.

1. Preheat the oven to 180°C (350°F/Gas 4). Oil the muffin moulds, or insert a paper case into each.

2. Sift the flour with the cocoa and baking powders into a bowl. Whisk the oil with the eggs and honey, add to the flour mix and beat with a balloon whisk until well combined.

3. Spoon the batter into the muffin moulds or cases. Stir the cherry purée in a saucepan with the icing sugar and cherry juice and bring to the boil. Dip the cherries in briefly and divide between the muffins, pressing in lightly. Reserve a few for decoration.

4. Bake the muffins on the middle shelf of the preheated oven for around 30 minutes. Do not open the oven door during this time. Remove from the oven and rest them in the tin for around 5 minutes. Then lift out the muffins and leave them to cool on a wire rack. To serve, dust with cocoa powder or icing sugar and top with the reserved cherries.

▼

BANANA CUPCAKES

with praline cream

For the praline cream: 70g (2½oz) almond brittle • 225g (8oz) double cream • 20g (¾oz) liquid glucose
For the cake: 70ml (2½fl oz) flavourless vegetable oil, plus extra for the moulds (optional) • 2–3 bananas, about 225g
(8oz) in total • 225g (8oz) caster sugar • 2 eggs • 225g (8oz) plain flour • 2 tsp baking powder • 60ml (2fl oz) milk
• 25g (scant 1oz) cocoa powder • 200g (7oz) nougat • 2 tbsp oats • 1 tbsp icing sugar • dried banana chips,
for decoration (optional) • Chocolate Sauce (optional, see p145)
Equipment: 12-hole muffin tray • 12 paper muffin cases (optional) • piping bag with star nozzle

Makes 12   Prep: 40 mins + 24 hrs chilling + cooling   Baking time: 35 mins

1. Prepare the praline cream a day in advance. Cut the almond brittle into pieces. Put 75g (2½oz) of the cream into a saucepan with the glucose and bring to the boil, add the brittle and use a hand-held blender to mix everything until it is smooth. Let the mixture cool until it is lukewarm, then stir in the remaining cream. Cover the praline cream and refrigerate for at least 24 hours.

2. The following day, preheat the oven to 180°C (350°F/Gas 4). Oil the muffin moulds, or insert a paper case into each.

3. Purée the bananas in a high-sided beaker with the hand-held blender. Whisk the caster sugar with the eggs in a bowl, using an electric hand whisk, until they are thick and creamy. Gradually pour in the oil in a thin stream, stirring all the time and continuing to mix until the ingredients have combined to form a cream with the consistency of mayonnaise. Fold the banana purée into the cream. Combine the flour with the baking powder and fold into the mixture, alternating with the milk.

4. Put around one-third of the mixture into a second bowl and stir in the cocoa powder. Chop the nougat into little pieces and stir into the other, lighter coloured mixture.

5. Spoon the cocoa mixture evenly between the muffin tray moulds or cases and top with the nougat mixture. Bake on the middle shelf of the preheated oven for around 35 minutes. Do not open the oven door during this time. Remove from the oven and let them rest in the tin for around another 5 minutes. Then lift out the cupcakes and leave them to cool on a wire rack.

6. To finish off, whip the chilled praline cream with an electric hand whisk on a medium-low speed until it is stiff; take care not to over-whisk, or the cream will begin to curdle. Put the cream into a piping bag fitted with a star nozzle and pipe onto the cupcakes. Caramelize the oats with the icing sugar in a pan. Sprinkle over the cupcakes and decorate with dried banana chips and chocolate sauce (if you like).

▼

STRAWBERRY CUPCAKES

with white chocolate ganache

For the ganache: 200g (7oz) double cream • 1 tsp liquid glucose • 125g (4½oz) white chocolate
For the cake: 100g (3½oz) unsalted butter, at room temperature, plus extra for the moulds (optional)
• 165g (5¾oz) strawberries, fresh or thawed from frozen, plus 250g (9oz) fresh strawberries, for decoration
• 165g (5¾oz) buttermilk • 80g (2¾oz) caster sugar • seeds from 1 vanilla pod • pinch of salt • 2 eggs
• 265g (9½oz) plain flour • 2 tsp baking powder • icing sugar, for dusting
For the crumble: 210g (7½oz) plain flour • 115g (4oz) demerara sugar • ½ tsp vanilla powder
• 100g (3½oz) unsalted butter, chilled and chopped
Equipment: 12-hole muffin tray • 12 paper muffin cases (optional) • piping bag with star nozzle

Makes 12   Prep: 20 mins + 24 hrs chilling + cooling   Baking time: 40–45 mins

1. A day in advance, make the chocolate ganache. Put 125g (4½oz) of the cream in a saucepan with the glucose. Bring to the boil. Chop the chocolate and place in a heatproof bowl. Pour the hot cream over the chocolate and leave for 2 minutes. Mix until smooth using a hand-held blender, while gradually adding the remaining (cold) cream. Cover and refrigerate for 24 hours.

2. The following day, preheat the oven to 180°C (350°F/Gas 4). Butter the muffin moulds, or insert a paper case into each.

3. Use a hand-held blender to purée the 165g (5¾oz) strawberries with the buttermilk in a high-sided beaker. Cream the butter with half the caster sugar, the vanilla seeds, and salt in a bowl, using an electric hand whisk, until light and fluffy. Separate the eggs. Add the egg yolks one at a time to the butter mix, beating after each addition until well combined. Stir in the strawberry purée.

4. Combine the flour with the baking powder and stir into the mixture just enough to combine. Beat

the egg whites in a bowl using the scrupulously cleaned electric hand whisk until stiff, gradually adding the remaining caster sugar as you go. Carefully fold into the batter, one-third at a time.

5. Spoon the mixture between the muffin moulds. Bake on the middle shelf of the preheated oven for 30–35 minutes until golden brown. Do not open the oven door during this time. Remove from the oven and leave to cool in the tin.

6. Meanwhile, for the crumble, rub together all the ingredients with your fingertips until the mixture looks like medium breadcrumbs. Line a baking tray with baking parchment, sprinkle evenly with the crumble, and bake alongside the cupcakes for around 8 minutes until golden.

7. Carefully beat the chilled ganache once more, on a medium speed, and spoon into a piping bag fitted with a star nozzle. Decorate the cupcakes first with the ganache, then with the crumble. Hull the strawberries and halve or quarter any large fruits. Use to decorate the cupcakes, dusting with icing sugar.

▼

ADVOCAAT CUPCAKES

Makes 12   Prep: 40 mins + 24 hrs chilling + cooling   Baking time: 30 mins

For the advocaat cream: 145g (5¼oz) white chocolate, plus white chocolate curls, for decoration • 1 tsp cocoa butter (from health food shops) • 165g (5¾oz) double cream • 100ml (3½fl oz) advocaat • 1 tsp liquid glucose
For the caramel: 165g (5¾oz) caster sugar • 100g (3½oz) extra thick double cream • 2 tbsp advocaat
For the cakes: 75g (2½oz) unsalted butter, at room temperature, plus extra for the moulds (optional)
• 60g (2oz) caster sugar • seeds from ½ vanilla pod • pinch of salt • 2 small eggs • 175ml (6fl oz) advocaat
• 50g (1¾oz) plain yogurt • 200g (7oz) wholemeal flour • 1½ tsp baking powder • icing sugar, for dusting
Equipment: 12-hole muffin tray • 12 paper muffin cases (optional) • piping bag with star nozzle

If you gently warm the cream for the caramel before adding it to the sugar,
it will be even quicker to prepare.

1. Make the advocaat cream a day in advance. Finely chop the chocolate and put into a heatproof bowl with the cocoa butter. Put 65g (2¼oz) of the cream into a saucepan with the advocaat and glucose and bring to the boil. Pour over the chocolate mixture, leave for 2 minutes, then stir with a spatula until melted. Stir in the remaining cream until smooth, then cover and refrigerate for 24 hours.

2. Make the caramel a day in advance as well. Lightly caramelize the sugar for the caramel in a saucepan over a moderate heat. Add the cream and advocaat and let the mixture simmer until the sugar has completely dissolved again. Let the caramel cool down, cover and refrigerate.

3. The following day, preheat the oven to 180°C (350°F/Gas 4). Butter the muffin moulds, or insert a paper case into each.

4. For the cakes, cream the butter with half the caster sugar, the vanilla seeds, and the salt in a bowl using an electric hand whisk until it is light and fluffy. Separate the eggs. Add the egg yolks one at a time to the butter and sugar mixture, beating after each addition just until all the ingredients are well combined. Finally, stir in the advocaat and yogurt.

5. Combine the flour with the baking powder then stir into the mixture just enough to produce a smooth consistency. Use the scrupulously cleaned electric hand whisk to beat the egg whites in a bowl until stiff, gradually adding the remaining sugar and whisking to combine after every addition. Carefully fold them into the batter, one-third at a time.

6. Spoon the batter into the muffin tray moulds or cases. Bake the cupcakes on the middle shelf of the preheated oven for around 30 minutes until golden brown. Remove from the oven and allow to cool for a further 5 minutes in the tin. Then lift out the cupcakes and leave them to cool on a wire rack.

7. To finish the cupcakes, whip the chilled advocaat cream using an electric hand whisk until it is stiff. As soon as the cream begins to hold its shape, stir in the caramel and continue to whisk only until the mixture is firm and smooth; don't whisk for too long or the mix will curdle. Transfer the cream into a piping bag fitted with a star nozzle and pipe onto the cupcakes. Decorate with the white chocolate curls and dust with icing sugar.

▼

WALNUT AND RED WINE MUFFINS

with fresh grapes

For the red wine reduction: 300ml (½ pint) red wine
For the cakes: 165g (5¾oz) unsalted butter, at room temperature, plus extra for the moulds (optional)
• 140g (5oz) caster sugar • 1 tsp vanilla powder • 3 small eggs • 165g (5¾oz) plain flour • 2½ tsp baking powder
• 1 tsp ground cinnamon • 1 tbsp cocoa powder • 65g (2¼oz) ground walnuts, plus 50g (1¾oz) walnut halves,
for decoration • 165ml (5½fl oz) red wine • 2 tbsp icing sugar • grapes, for decoration
Equipment: 12-hole muffin tray • 12 paper muffin cases (optional)

Makes 12   Prep: 40 mins + cooling   Baking time: 25 mins

1. Boil the red wine for the red wine reduction until it reduces to a viscous consistency. Set aside.

2. Preheat the oven to 180°C (350°F/Gas 4). Butter the muffin moulds, or insert a paper case into each.

3. Cream the butter, caster sugar, and vanilla powder in a bowl using an electric hand whisk until pale and fluffy. Add the eggs one at a time, beating after each addition just enough to ensure that the ingredients are well combined. Mix the flour with the baking powder, cinnamon, cocoa powder, and ground walnuts and stir into the mixture, alternating with the red wine.

4. Spoon the batter into the muffin tray moulds or cases. Bake the muffins on the middle shelf of the preheated oven for around 25 minutes. Do not open the oven door during this time. Remove from the oven and allow to cool for a further 5 minutes in the tin. Then lift out the muffins and leave them to cool on a wire rack.

5. Toast the walnut halves for decoration on a baking tray lined with baking parchment in an oven preheated to 180°C (350°F/Gas 4) for 3–4 minutes until golden brown. Remove and leave to cool down. Then sprinkle them with the icing sugar in a saucepan and allow to caramelize over a moderate heat. Roughly chop. Halve the grapes.

6. To finish the muffins, drizzle with the cooled, sticky red wine reduction and decorate with the caramelized walnuts and halved grapes.

Tip: choosing the wine
These muffins are ideal to serve at a drinks party. Just use the wine that you are going to offer at the party in the baking. Experiment with the flavours and intensities of your favourite wines. Even if you feel they don't stand out particularly distinctly in the muffins, they will still have a subtle effect.

▼

WHITE CHOCOLATE MUFFINS

with beetroot

For the muffins: 40g (1¼oz) unsalted butter, plus extra for the moulds (optional) • 140g (5oz) ready-cooked beetroot, in natural juices (not vinegar!) • 100g (3½oz) white chocolate • 200g (7oz) plain flour • 80g (2¼oz) rye flour • 2 tsp baking powder • 125g (4½oz) caster sugar • 2 tsp vanilla powder • 200ml (7fl oz) milk • 2 eggs • 3 tbsp beetroot juice (from the jar)
For the glazed beetroot and decoration: 250ml (9fl oz) beetroot juice (from the jar) • ½ sachet vanilla blancmange mix • 50g (1¾oz) caster sugar • 200g (7oz) ready-cooked beetroot, in natural juices • ready-made glacé or poured fondant icing, for decoration (see p219)
Equipment: 12-hole muffin tray • 12 paper muffin cases (optional) • small piping bag (optional)

Makes 12   Prep: 20 mins + cooling   Baking time: 25–30 mins

In this muffin I combine the sweet-and-sour earthiness of beetroot with the intense sweetness of white chocolate. They make perfect companions because the sweet flavour of the chocolate compensates for the tartness of the beet, while simultaneously bringing out the vegetable's sweet notes. What's more, the colour is an absolute winner.

1. Preheat the oven to 180°C (350°F/Gas 4). Butter the muffin moulds, or insert a paper case into each.

2. To make the muffins, chop the beetroot finely. Melt the butter in a saucepan over a low heat. Chop the white chocolate finely and melt it with the butter. Combine the flours and baking powder.

3. Beat the sugar, vanilla powder, milk, and eggs in a bowl using an electric hand whisk. Stir in the beetroot juice. Fold in the chocolate mixture, then the flour mixture, and finally the beetroot.

4. Divide the batter between the moulds or cases. Bake on the middle shelf of the preheated oven for 25–30 minutes. Remove from the oven and let them rest in the tin for 5 minutes. Then lift out the muffins and leave them to cool on a wire rack.

5. To make the glaze, stir 3–4 tbsp of beetroot juice into the blancmange mix until smooth, boil up the rest of the juice with the sugar and add the blancmange mix. Stamp out 1–2cm (½–¾in) circles from the beetroot slices and use a fork to dip these in the glaze, letting any excess drip off. Decorate each muffin with around 3 beetroot circles. Use a piping bag or spoon to drizzle on fine lines of icing.

▼

RICE PUDDING MUFFINS

with cherries

For the muffins: 25g (scant 1oz) unsalted butter, at room temperature, plus extra for the moulds (optional)
• 25g (scant 1oz) unsalted rice cakes (from health food shops) • 2 eggs • seeds from 1 vanilla pod • 110g (3¾oz)
caster sugar • 100g (3½oz) plain flour • 50g (1¾oz) rice flour • 2 tsp baking powder • 1 heaped tsp ground cinnamon
• 125ml (4fl oz) milk • 40g (1¼oz) sour cherries, pitted, thawed from frozen • 125g (4½oz) cooked rice pudding
(bought or home-made, see tip)
For the decoration: 75g (2½oz) unsalted rice cakes • 2 tbsp icing sugar • 2 tsp cornflour • 2 tsp caster sugar
• 100ml (3½fl oz) cherry juice • 1 cinnamon stick • 125g (4½oz) sour cherries, pitted; fresh, or thawed from frozen
Equipment: 12-hole muffin tray • 12 paper muffin cases (optional) • piping bag with medium round nozzle

Makes 12   Prep: 40 mins + cooling   Baking time: 25 mins

1. Preheat the oven to 180°C (350°F/Gas 4). Butter the muffin moulds, or insert a paper case into each.

2. To make the muffins, roughly chop the rice cakes. Cream the butter and eggs in a bowl with an electric hand whisk until light and fluffy. Stir in the vanilla seeds and sugar. Combine the flour, rice flour, baking powder, and cinnamon, and add to the butter mixture alternating with the milk. Finally, fold in the rice cake pieces, cherries, and rice pudding.

3. Divide the batter evenly between the moulds or cases. Bake on the middle shelf of the preheated oven for around 25 minutes until golden brown. Remove from the oven and leave to cool in the tin.

4. For decoration, first break up the rice cakes to the size you desire. Heat a saucepan, add the rice cake pieces, scatter with the icing sugar, and let them caramelize over a medium heat, turning constantly. Remove from the pan and set aside. Mix the

cornflour with the caster sugar and 2 tbsp of the cherry juice and stir until smooth. Bring the remaining cherry juice to the boil in a saucepan with the cinnamon stick. Add the cherries and simmer for 2 minutes, stirring all the time. Stir in the cornflour mixture and let everything return to the boil briefly. Allow to cool down, removing the cinnamon stick. Decorate the muffins with the cherry mixture and caramelized rice cake pieces.

Tip: vary the rice pudding
These also taste great if you vary the flavour of the rice pudding, for example with cinnamon and sugar, or banana, or chocolate.

Tip: making rice pudding
Makes around 150 g (5½oz) rice pudding. Bring to the boil 125ml (4fl oz) milk with 30g (1oz) pudding rice and a pinch of salt, cover, and cook over a low heat for around 20 minutes, stirring occasionally. Leave to cool. Shop-bought rice pudding tends to have a runnier consistency than home-made, so, if necessary, reduce the quantity of milk in the muffin mix to 110ml (3¾fl oz).

Tip: a touch of caramel
These are delicious if you add
2 tbsp of caramel syrup (such as
from Monin) to the cream. Stir
it into the milk mixture before
you add the gelatine.

▼

MILK SLICES

with chocolate sponge

For the sponge: 200g (7oz) plain flour • 40g (1¼oz) cocoa powder • 8 eggs • 160g (5¾oz) caster sugar • 2 tsp vanilla powder • 2 pinches of salt
For the filling: 7 leaves of gelatine • 500ml (18fl oz) milk • 30g (1oz) cornflour • 50g (1¾oz) powdered milk • 120g (4¼oz) caster sugar • 500g (1lb 2oz) double cream
Equipment: large 60 × 40cm (24 × 16in) baking tray (optional)

Makes 12   Prep: 30 mins + 3 hrs chilling + cooling   Baking time: 8 mins

1. Preheat the oven to 180°C (350°F/Gas 4). Line the large baking tray, or 2 regular baking trays, with baking parchment. Sift the flour with the cocoa.

2. Beat the eggs with 2 tbsp of water, the sugar, vanilla powder, and salt in a bowl using an electric hand whisk until they are light and creamy. Carefully fold the flour mixture into the egg mixture. Spread evenly over the baking tray or trays, smooth it out, and bake on the middle shelf of the preheated oven for around 8 minutes.

3. Remove from the oven, turn it out immediately onto a sheet of baking parchment and remove the baking parchment on which the sponge was baked. Leave to cool, covered with a clean tea towel.

4. Meanwhile, soak the gelatine for the filling in cold water for 10 minutes. Use a hand-held blender to mix the milk, cornflour, powdered milk, and sugar in a saucepan until smooth. Bring the mixture to the boil and let it simmer for a couple of minutes,

stirring continuously with a balloon whisk. Squeeze out the gelatine and dissolve it in the warmed milk. Cover the surface with cling film, then refrigerate to set for around 2 hours.

5. Use a balloon whisk to stir the filling until it is smooth. Whip the cream in a bowl until stiff, using an electric hand whisk on a medium setting, then gradually fold into the filling.

6. If you baked a large chocolate sponge, cut it in half to get 2 pieces each measuring 30 × 20cm (12 × 8in). Spread the filling on a sponge slab, place the other piece of sponge on top and press down lightly. Refrigerate for around 1 hour, then cut into 12 slices with a serrated knife. Don't press down when you are cutting, or the filling will squeeze out of the sides.

▼

CHOCOLATE CHIP COOKIES

with nuts

400g (14oz) dark chocolate • 150g (5½oz) walnuts • 210g (7½oz) unsalted butter, at room temperature • 200g (7oz) icing sugar • pinch of salt • 2 eggs • 350g (12oz) plain flour • 3 tsp baking powder • 150g (5½oz) chopped hazelnuts

Makes about 30   Prep: 25 mins + 2 hrs chilling + cooling   Baking time: 20–30 mins

I cannot imagine there is anyone in the world who doesn't like chocolate chip cookies. They are an absolute classic. When you first take a bite they are crisp, then the chocolate chunks provide that mouth-watering melting sensation. Simple perfection.

1. Roughly chop the chocolate and walnuts. Cream the butter with the icing sugar and salt in a bowl using an electric hand whisk until smooth. Beat in the eggs one at a time, until all the ingredients are well combined.

2. Mix the flour with the baking powder, walnuts, and hazelnuts. Stir the flour mixture into the cookie mix just enough to combine. Finally, knead in the chopped chocolate.

3. Roll the dough out on a piece of cling film to form a log; its thickness can be varied depending on the size of cookies you want. Wrap securely with the cling film, twist the ends to seal, then refrigerate for around 2 hours.

4. Preheat the oven to 190°C (375°F/Gas 5) and line a baking tray with baking parchment. Cut the chilled dough roll into slices around 2cm (¾in) thick. Lay these slices on the baking tray, reforming them slightly so they are round in shape, and leaving a 1–2cm (½–¾in) gap between each.

5. Bake the cookies on the middle shelf of the preheated oven for 20–30 minutes, depending on how thick they are. Remove from the oven and leave to cool on a wire rack.

▼

WALNUT COOKIES

with bananas

180g (6oz) walnuts • 100g (3½oz) fully ripe (blackened) bananas • 100g (3½oz) dried banana chips • 220g (8oz) plain flour • 1 tsp baking powder • pinch of salt • 150g (5½oz) unsalted butter, at room temperature • 200g (7oz) light brown sugar • 1 egg • pinch of ground cinnamon • 1 tsp vanilla powder • 2 tsp milk • icing sugar, for dusting

Makes about 15   Prep: 25 mins + 12 hrs freezing + cooling   Baking time: 10–15 mins

1. Preheat the oven to 180°C (350°F/Gas 4). Spread the walnuts on a baking tray and toast on the middle shelf of the oven for around 10 minutes. Remove from the tray, leave to cool, then chop finely. Cut the bananas into very small cubes. Finely chop the dried banana chips. Mix the flour with the baking powder and salt.

2. Beat the butter and light brown sugar in a bowl with an electric hand whisk until creamy. Beat in the egg, then the cinnamon, vanilla powder, and milk. Use a spatula to work in the fresh and dried banana pieces, the walnuts and the flour mixture.

3. Roll the dough out on a piece of cling film to form a log about 30cm (12in) long. Wrap securely with the cling film, twist the ends to seal, then leave in the freezer for around 12 hours.

4. Preheat the oven again to 180°C (350°F/Gas 4). Line a baking tray with baking parchment. Slice the frozen dough roll into 2cm (¾in) thick slices. Lay the slices on the baking tray, leaving a 1–2cm (½–¾in) gap between each.

5. Bake the cookies on the middle shelf of the preheated oven for 10–15 minutes, depending on thickness, until they are golden brown; they should still be somewhat softer in the middle. Remove from the oven and leave them to cool on a wire rack. Dust with icing sugar to serve.

▼

HAZELNUT AND APPLE COOKIES

with a hint of caramel

100g (3½oz) apple (peeled weight) • 100g (3½oz) dried apple rings • 150g (5½oz) unsalted butter, at room temperature • 200g (7oz) light brown sugar • 1 egg • 1 tsp ground cinnamon • 1 tsp vanilla powder • 4 tbsp milk • 220g (8oz) plain flour • 1 tsp baking powder • pinch of salt • 140g (5oz) finely chopped hazelnuts • 50g (1¾oz) oats

Makes about 15   Prep: 25 mins + 2 hrs chilling + cooling   Baking time: 20 mins

1. Chop the apple into very small pieces and finely chop the dried apple rings.

2. Cream the butter with the sugar in a bowl using an electric hand whisk until it is light and fluffy. Stir in the egg until well combined. Add the cinnamon, vanilla powder, and milk. Combine the flour with the baking powder and salt. Add the flour mixture to the butter and sugar mix along with the fresh and dried apple pieces, hazelnuts, and oats. Knead all the ingredients together to make a soft dough.

3. Roll the dough on a piece of cling film to form a log about 30cm (12in) long; make it thicker for larger cookies, if you prefer, or thinner for smaller cookies. Wrap securely with the cling film, twist the ends to seal, then leave in the freezer for around 2 hours.

4. Preheat the oven to 190°C (375°F/Gas 5). Line a baking tray with baking parchment. Remove the dough roll from the freezer and cut into slices around 2cm (¾in) thick. Lay the slices on the baking tray, leaving a 1–2cm (½–¾in) gap between each.

5. Bake the cookies on the middle shelf of the preheated oven for around 20 minutes, depending on their thickness. Remove from the oven and leave to cool on a wire rack.

Tip: *freezing cookie dough*
If you want to be prepared for unexpected visitors, you can freeze a cookie dough roll. When required, cut as many slices as you want from the frozen roll for baking. Return the remaining dough to the freezer for another time.

▼

MACADAMIA CARAMEL COOKIES

with Maldon salt

Makes about 15
Prep: 40 mins + 12 hrs freezing + cooling
Baking time: 15 mins

For the caramelized nuts: 200g (7oz) macadamia nuts • 2 tbsp icing sugar
For the cookies: 150g (5½oz) unsalted butter, at room temperature • 200g (7oz) light brown sugar • 1 egg
• 4 tbsp milk • ½ tsp vanilla powder • seeds from 1 vanilla pod • ½ tsp Maldon salt, plus extra for decoration
• 220g (8oz) plain flour • 1 tsp baking powder
For the caramel sauce: 125g (4½oz) caster sugar • 125g (4½oz) double cream • 15g (½oz) unsalted butter

1. To make the caramelized nuts, preheat the oven to 180°C (350°F/Gas 4). Spread the macadamia nuts on a baking tray and toast on the middle shelf of the oven for around 10 minutes, then remove from the tray and leave to cool. Put the nuts in a saucepan, sprinkle with the icing sugar and caramelize them evenly over a medium heat, stirring constantly. Let the nuts cool on a chopping board, then transfer to a freezer bag, crush with a rolling pin and set aside.

2. For the cookies, beat the butter and light brown sugar in a bowl using an electric hand whisk until creamy. Beat in the egg, milk, vanilla powder, vanilla seeds, and salt. Mix the flour with the baking powder and stir this in, too. Finally, fold in the caramelized nuts, reserving a few for decoration.

3. Roll the dough out on a piece of cling film to form a log about 30cm (12in) long; make it thicker for larger cookies, or thinner for smaller cookies. Wrap securely with the cling film, twist the ends to seal, then leave in the freezer for around 12 hours.

4. Preheat the oven again to 180°C (350°F/Gas 4) and line a baking tray with baking parchment. Cut the frozen dough roll into slices around 2cm (¾in) thick. Lay the slices on the tray, leaving a 1–2cm (½–¾in) gap between each.

5. Bake on the middle shelf in the preheated oven for about 15 minutes, until crisp and golden brown. Remove from the oven. Leave to cool on a wire rack.

6. Meanwhile, caramelize the caster sugar for the caramel sauce in a saucepan over a medium heat. Pour in the cream and let cook gently over a medium-low heat, stirring occasionally until the solid pieces of caramel have dissolved. Finally, mix in the butter with a hand-held blender. Leave the sauce to cool. Cover and refrigerate until ready to use.

7. To serve, use a teaspoon or a small piping bag to drizzle some of the caramel sauce in any pattern you like on the cookies. Decorate each with 1–2 flakes of Maldon salt and a few of the reserved caramelized nuts. Any leftover caramel sauce can be kept refrigerated for up to 1 month.

Tip: high class sea salt
In Essex, a particularly aromatic sea salt called Maldon salt is produced. It has a firm, crunchy consistency, making it ideal for sophisticated baking. While it is somewhat more expensive than other sea salt, it is worth trying for these cookies.

▼

COOKIE SANDWICH

with salted chocolate cream

For the biscuits: 35g (1¼oz) unsalted butter, at room temperature • 80g (2¾oz) icing sugar • 1 egg
• 30g (1oz) ground almonds • 225g (9oz) plain flour, plus extra for dusting • 1 tsp vanilla powder
• seeds from ½ vanilla pod • finely grated zest of 1 orange • finely grated zest of 1 unwaxed lemon
For the filling and decoration: 300g (10oz) dark chocolate (60% cocoa solids) • 25g (scant 1oz) double cream
• 75g (2½oz) liquid glucose • 200g (7oz) unsalted butter, chopped • sea salt flakes, for decoration
Equipment: 5cm (2in) fluted cutter (optional) • piping bag with large round nozzle (optional)

Makes about 20   Prep: 30 mins + 2 hrs chilling + cooling   Baking time: 10–15 mins

1. To make the biscuits, mix the butter, icing sugar, and egg in the bowl of a mixer fitted with a dough hook. Add the almonds, flour, vanilla powder, vanilla seeds, and orange and lemon zests and work everything swiftly to a smooth consistency. Shape into a ball, press it flat, wrap in cling film and refrigerate for at least 2 hours.

2. Finely chop the chocolate for the filling. Bring the cream to the boil in a saucepan with the glucose. Stir in the chocolate and let it melt. Gradually stir in the butter. Leave to cool, then cover and refrigerate for at least 2 hours.

3. Preheat the oven to 180°C (350°F/Gas 4). Line a baking tray with baking parchment. Roll out the biscuit dough on a lightly floured work surface to 5mm (¼in) thick. Use the cutter or a glass to stamp out 5cm (2in) circles, lay them on the tray and bake them on the middle shelf of the preheated oven for

10–15 minutes until they are light brown and crisp. Remove from the oven and leave to cool on a wire rack.

4. Spoon the filling into a piping bag fitted with a large round nozzle (if using). Pipe some onto half the biscuits or, alternatively, just use a spoon to dollop on some of the mix before spreading it. Sprinkle very lightly with sea salt flakes, top with a second biscuit, and press down gently.

▼

MOLTEN CHOCOLATE CAKES

with fondant centres

For the molten centres: **45g (1½oz) unsalted butter** • **200g (7oz) very dark chocolate (80% cocoa solids)** • **125g (4½oz) double cream** • **35g (1¼oz) liquid glucose**
For the cakes: **320g (11oz) dark chocolate (70% cocoa solids)** • **300g (10oz) unsalted butter** • **10 eggs** • **300g (10oz) caster sugar** • **130g (4½oz) plain flour**
Equipment: **silicone hemisphere 20-hole baking mould (each mould 3–4cm / 1¼–1½in in diameter), or a similar-sized ice cube tray** • **20 ovenproof glass ramekins, 6cm (2½in) deep** • **piping bag with large round nozzle (optional)**

Makes about 20   Prep: 20 mins + 1 hr freezing   Baking time: 7–10 mins

1. To make the molten centres, chop the butter and chocolate finely. Put both into a heatproof bowl. Bring the cream to the boil in a saucepan with the glucose, pour over the chocolate and butter mix and slowly stir with a balloon whisk until you have a smooth consistency. Pour the chocolate mix into the cavities of the silicone mould or ice cube tray, cover, and then freeze.

2. Finely chop the chocolate and butter for the cakes. Melt them both together in a heatproof bowl placed over simmering water; the bowl should not touch the water.

3. Beat the eggs and sugar in a bowl using an electric hand whisk until they are slightly frothy. Gradually stir in the chocolate mixture. Finally, fold in the flour.

4. Preheat the oven to 190°C (375°F/Gas 5). Divide the mixture evenly between the ramekins, ideally by using a piping bag fitted with a large round nozzle. Press a frozen chocolate centre into each so that it is completely covered by the mixture.

5. Place the ramekins on a baking tray and bake on the middle shelf of the hot oven for 7–10 minutes. Remove and serve when lukewarm.

Tip: perfect for guests
These are ideal when catering for lots of guests. The mix can be prepared up to 3 days in advance, put into the ramekins and then stored, covered, in the refrigerator. To finish off, just press in the frozen centres and bake the cakes for a couple of minutes longer than specified, due to the mix being chilled before baking.

▼

WAFFLES

Belgian style

For the waffles: 150g (5½oz) unsalted butter • 90ml (3fl oz) milk • 20g (¾oz) fresh yeast • 200g (7oz) plain flour • 100g (3½oz) light rye flour • 2 eggs • pinch of salt • 1½ tbsp vanilla powder • 125g (4½oz) pearl sugar (see p218) • flavourless vegetable oil, for cooking (optional) • icing sugar, for dusting
Equipment: **waffle maker**

Makes about 8   Prep: 15 mins   Baking time: 30 mins

Waffles are the ultimate childhood memory for me. The simple waffles my mother made were absolutely delicious, but over time I have discovered that I'm particularly fond of the thick Belgian variety. They are denser and have a quite different mouthfeel.

1. Melt the butter in a saucepan over a low heat. Heat the milk in a separate pan with 90ml (3fl oz) of water until it is lukewarm and dissolve the yeast in it. Mix together both types of flour in a large bowl.

2. Beat the eggs, salt, and vanilla powder in a bowl using an electric hand whisk until foamy. Stir in the milk mixture, then the combined flours. Gradually pour in the butter, stirring all the time. Finally, fold in the pearl sugar.

3. Preheat the waffle maker. If necessary, lightly oil the baking surfaces. Pour 2 tbsp of the batter onto the baking surface, close the waffle maker and cook for 2–3 minutes. Bake golden brown waffles from your mixture until it is all used up. Serve warm, dusted with icing sugar.

Tip: pile them high
Create a waffle 'torte' by simply layering up waffles with cream (or a flavoured cream) and cherries or plums.

▼

CRUNCHY NOUGAT

with a chocolate glaze

For the crunchy nougat: **flavourless vegetable oil, for the tray** • **50g (1¾oz) ground almonds**
• **600g (1lb 5oz) caster sugar** • **500g (1lb 2oz) almond nougat**
For the glaze: **150g (5½oz) almond brittle** • **150g (5½oz) dark chocolate**
Equipment: **sugar thermometer** • **decorating comb (optional)**

Makes about 20 pieces   Prep: 30 mins + 1 hr chilling + heating

1. For the crunchy nougat, preheat the oven to 100°C (210°F/Gas ¼). Oil a baking tray and warm it in the oven. Sprinkle a sheet of baking parchment evenly with ground almonds.

2. Lightly caramelize the sugar in a saucepan over a medium heat. At the same time, melt the nougat to 80°C (175°F) in a heatproof bowl placed over simmering water (don't allow the bowl to touch the water). Remove the hot baking tray from the oven and first pour on the sugar, then the melted nougat.

3. Fold the sugar and nougat together using 2 spatulas, tossing them over each other several times so you get several layers of sugar and nougat. Pour onto the baking parchment with the almonds and toss everything together. Place another sheet of baking parchment on top and roll the mixture out to form a rectangular slab around 2cm (¾in) thick. Let it cool down to room temperature.

4. For the glaze, chop the brittle and chocolate finely. Melt together in a heatproof bowl over simmering water (don't allow the bowl to touch the water). Spread half in an even thin layer over the cooled nougat. Refrigerate for 30 minutes until set.

5. Turn the nougat slab over. If the remaining glaze has set, melt it again over the simmering water and spread it over the nougat slab. If you like, use a decorating comb to create a wave pattern in the glaze. Refrigerate again for 30 minutes to set.

6. Remove the slab from the refrigerator 20 minutes before serving to let it return to room temperature. With a sharp knife, cut into 3 × 3cm (1¼ × 1¼in) pieces. If wrapped in cling film, the crunchy nougat can be kept refrigerated for about 1 week.

Tip: simple variants
This is quicker to make with ready-made praline paste and pailleté feuilletine which you can buy via mail order (see p218). Melt 375g (13oz) praline paste (60% hazelnut) with 150g (5½oz) milk chocolate in a heatproof bowl over simmering water (don't let the bowl touch the water). Mix in 180g (8oz) pailleté feuilletine. Spread out in a 2cm (¾in) thick layer on a baking tray lined with baking parchment. Leave to set in the refrigerator for 4 hours. Then coat with the glaze and cut into pieces as instructed.

▼

COCONUT GINGER MACAROONS

with chilli

For the macaroons: 10g (¼oz) fresh root ginger • 240g (8¾oz) caster sugar • 170g (6oz) egg whites (from about 5 eggs) • 200g (7oz) desiccated coconut • pinch of chilli powder (see tip) • white chocolate, melted (optional) • dark chocolate, melted (optional) • angel hair (shredded and dried) chilli (optional, see p218)
Equipment: piping bag with a medium round nozzle

Makes about 50   Prep: 15 mins + cooling   Baking time: 15 mins

I developed these macaroons to be eaten at the end of an Asian meal. They are truly special: the mild coconut, the fresh edge of the ginger, and the characteristic heat of the chilli.

1. Preheat the oven to 180°C (350°F/Gas 4). Line a baking tray with baking parchment. Peel and finely chop the ginger.

2. Combine the ginger, sugar, egg whites, desiccated coconut, and chilli powder in a heatproof bowl. Place over simmering water, stirring until it looks slightly glossy (don't let the bowl touch the water, or get too hot).

3. Spoon into a piping bag fitted with a medium round nozzle and pipe out 50 little mounds, each about 3cm (1¼in) in diameter, onto the baking tray.

4. Bake the macaroons on the middle shelf of the preheated oven for around 15 minutes until golden brown. Remove and leave to cool on a wire rack. If desired, decorate with melted chocolate and angel hair chilli.

Tip: add chilli powder with care!
Depending on the producer and the composition, the heat of each batch of chilli powder will vary. So add the chilli very carefully at first and keep tasting the mix until it has a level of heat with which you are comfortable.

Tip: get stocked up
Amaretti are ideally suited for preparing in advance. Whether it's winter or summer, they retain their consistency for a long time and will keep for 2–3 weeks packed in an airtight container. The same is true of Cantuccini (see p56).

▼

AMARETTI

with fragrant almonds

For the amaretti: **4 egg whites, plus 1 egg yolk** • **pinch of salt** • **seeds from 1 vanilla pod** • **200g (7oz) icing sugar, plus extra for dusting (optional)** • **400g (14oz) ground almonds** • **6 tbsp amaretto** • **1 tbsp lemon juice**
Equipment: **piping bag with medium round nozzle**

Makes about 50   Prep. 15 mins + cooling   Baking time: 1¼ hrs

Amaretti are classic little Italian biscuits which are wonderful eaten with espresso. The delicate almond flavour of amaretto makes them ideal for use in desserts such as trifle, with layers of cream and fruit.

1. Preheat the oven to 150°C (300°F/Gas2). Line a baking tray with baking parchment.

2. Beat the egg whites with the salt and vanilla seeds in a bowl, using an electric hand whisk, until stiff, gradually spooning in the icing sugar as you go (see tip, right). Gradually add the almonds, then carefully fold in the egg yolk, amaretto, and lemon juice.

3. Spoon the almond mixture into a piping bag fitted with a medium round nozzle and pipe about 50 small, even sized mounds, each 1–2cm (½–¾in) in diameter, onto the baking tray.

4. Bake the amaretti on the middle shelf of the preheated oven for around 15 minutes until golden brown, then switch off the oven and allow the

amaretti to dry out for 1 further hour in the switched-off oven. Finally, remove from the oven and leave to cool down on a wire rack.

5. If you like, dust the amaretti with a bit more icing sugar to serve. Store in an airtight, sealable container until ready for use.

Tip: whipping egg whites
It is crucial to set the electric hand whisk to a medium speed when beating the egg whites. This will mean the whisked whites are stable.

▼

CANTUCCINI

Italian style

250g (9oz) plain flour • 1 tsp baking powder • 140g (5oz) caster sugar • 50g (1¾oz) ground almonds • 2 eggs, plus 2 egg yolks • 120g (4¼oz) blanched whole almonds

Makes about 50   Prep: 25 mins + 20 mins chilling + cooling   Baking time: 40 mins

These little double-baked almond biscuits from Tuscany are best eaten alongside a glass of Vin Santo dessert wine, also from Italy, since it complements their sweetness particularly well. The double-baking means they are really crunchy and the perfect companion to coffee or tea.

1. Mix the flour and baking powder in the bowl of a mixer fitted with a dough hook, along with the sugar and ground almonds. Add the eggs and egg yolks and knead everything quickly to form a smooth dough. Briefly knead in the whole almonds. Shape the dough into a ball, wrap securely in cling film and let it rest in the refrigerator for 20 minutes.

2. In the meantime, preheat the oven to 180°C (350°F/Gas 4) and line a baking tray with baking parchment. Divide the dough into 5 pieces and shape each into a flattish log about 3cm (1¼in) in diameter. Lay the logs on athe baking tray, leaving a gap of around 5cm (2in) between each.

3. Bake the dough logs on the middle shelf of the preheated oven for around 25 minutes. Remove from the oven and let them cool down, but leave the oven on. Cut the baked rolls across at an angle into slices around 1cm (½in) thick with a serrated knife and lay these back on the baking tray. Bake the cantuccini in the oven for another 15 minutes until they are golden brown.

4. Take the cantuccini out of the oven and leave them to cool on a wire rack. Store in an airtight container until ready for use.

▼

CHOCOLATE TARTS

For the pastry: 150g (5½oz) unsalted butter, chopped, plus extra for the tins • 100g (3½oz) icing sugar
• 30g (1oz) ground almonds • 1 egg • 250g (9oz) plain flour, plus extra for dusting (optional)
For the filling: 240g (8½oz) very dark chocolate (80% cocoa solids) • 230g (8oz) double cream
• 25g (scant 1oz) liquid glucose • 40g (1¼oz) unsalted butter, chopped, at room temperature
Equipment: 2 x 12cm (5in) tartlet tins • baking beans, dried pulses, or raw rice

Makes 2   Prep: 30 mins + 4 hrs chilling + cooling   Baking time: 15–20 mins

1. To make the shortcrust pastry, mix the butter and icing sugar in a bowl. Either rub the butter into the sugar with your fingertips, or use a mixer fitted with a dough hook. Next, knead in the ground almonds, and then the egg. Finally, sift over the flour and work all the ingredients swiftly until smooth. Shape the pastry into a ball, press flat, wrap in cling film, and refrigerate for at least 2 hours.

2. Preheat the oven to 180°C (350°F/Gas 4) and butter the 2 tart tins. Roll out the pastry on a lightly floured work surface, or between 2 pieces of cling film, until it is about 5mm (¼in) thick, and use it to line the tins. Cut off any overhanging pastry edges and prick the pastry bases several times with a fork.

3. To bake blind, line the pastry cases with baking parchment and fill with baking beans, dried pulses, or raw rice, to weigh it down. Blind-bake the pastry cases on the middle shelf of the preheated oven for 10 minutes. Remove the baking beans, pulses, or rice, and the baking parchment, and continue to bake for a further 5–10 minutes until the tart bases are golden brown. Remove the pastry bases from the oven and let them cool in the tins.

4. Meanwhile, chop the chocolate for the filling into little pieces. Bring the cream and glucose to the boil in a saucepan. Remove from the hob and gradually add in the chocolate, while beating with a hand-held blender, taking care not to incorporate any air in the process. Mix in the butter, again making sure you don't incorporate any air.

5. Fill the tart cases with the chocolate mixture and smooth it out. Let them cool down uncovered at room temperature, then cover and refrigerate for at least 2 hours. To cut the tarts, use a knife with a hot blade: dip the knife blade briefly in hot water, wipe it dry, then immediately use to cut the tart.

Tip: regal gold and silver decoration
This tart looks particularly stunning if decorated with little pieces of gold or silver leaf, or with gold leaf flakes. These can be bought from larger supermarkets, or mail order companies (see p218), and will keep for ever.

▼

SOURED CREAM TARTS

simply ingenious

For the pastry: 135g (4¾oz) unsalted butter, chopped, plus extra for the tins • 80g (2¾oz) icing sugar • 1 egg • 1 tsp vanilla powder • pinch of salt • seeds from ¼ vanilla pod • 30g (1oz) ground almonds • 225g (8oz) plain flour, plus extra for the tins and for dusting
For the filling: 1 egg • 50g (1¾oz) caster sugar • 20g (¾oz) vanilla blancmange mix • 500g (1lb 2oz) soured cream • fresh blueberries, to serve (optional)

Equipment: 2 x 12cm (5in) tartlet tins • baking beans, dried pulses, or raw rice

Makes 2   Prep: 20 mins + 6 hrs chilling + cooling   Baking time: 35 mins

1. To make the shortcrust pastry, knead together the butter, sugar, egg, vanilla powder, salt, and vanilla seeds in the bowl of a mixer fitted with a dough hook. Add the almonds and flour and work everything swiftly to a smooth consistency. Shape the pastry into a ball, press flat, wrap in cling film and refrigerate for at least 2 hours.

2. Meanwhile, use a balloon whisk to combine the egg with the sugar, blancmange mix, and soured cream in a high-sided bowl, taking care not to incorporate any air. Preheat the oven to 190°C (375°F/Gas 5). Lightly butter the tartlet tins and dust with flour, knocking out any excess.

3. Roll out the pastry on a lightly floured work surface or between 2 pieces of cling film into a 5mm (¼in) thick circle, and use this to line the tins. Trim off overhanging pastry and prick all over with a fork.

4. Line the pastry cases with baking parchment and fill with baking beans to weigh it down for baking blind. Bake the pastry on the middle shelf of the preheated oven for around 15 minutes.

5. Remove the tins from the oven and take out the baking beans with the baking parchment. Pour the soured cream mixture onto the pastry bases and smooth it out. Return to the oven and bake for around 20 minutes on the middle shelf. The mixture should still wobble slightly in the centre as it will continue to set as it cools. Take out of the oven and let cool in the tins, then refrigerate for at least 4 hours. Take them carefully out of their tins and garnish with blueberries (if using), to serve.

▼

RED WINE CAKE

with Chantilly cream

For the cake: 250g (9oz) unsalted butter, at room temperature, plus extra for the tin • 250g (9oz) plain flour, plus extra for the tin • 2 tsp baking powder • 1 tbsp cocoa powder • 100g (3½oz) ground almonds • 200g (7oz) caster sugar • 2 tsp vanilla powder • 1 tbsp ground cinnamon • 4 eggs • 250ml (9fl oz) red wine, plus 150–200ml (5–7fl oz) for soaking • grapes, halved, for decoration • white chocolate, grated, for decoration • almond brittle, crushed, for decoration (optional)

For the Chantilly cream: 300g (10oz) extra thick double cream • 50g (1¾oz) double cream • 60g (2oz) icing sugar • seeds from 1 vanilla pod

Equipment: 24cm (9½in) springform tin • piping bag with round nozzle

Serves 12   Prep: 20 mins + cooling   Baking time: 45–50 mins

1. Preheat the oven to 180°C (350°F/Gas 4). Butter the cake tin, then dust it with flour, shaking out any excess. Mix the flour with the baking powder, cocoa powder, and ground almonds.

2. Cream the butter with the sugar, vanilla powder, and cinnamon in a bowl, using an electric hand whisk set to a medium speed, for around 5 minutes, until light and fluffy. Add the eggs one at a time, beating well after each addition. Mix in the 250ml (9fl oz) red wine and, finally, the flour mixture.

3. Spoon the cake batter into the tin and smooth it out. Bake the cake on the middle shelf of the preheated oven for 45–50 minutes.

4. For the Chantilly cream, use the electric hand whisk to beat the extra thick double cream, regular double cream, icing sugar, and vanilla seeds until it holds its shape. Spoon into a piping bag fitted with a round nozzle. Store in a cold place, but not the refrigerator, until ready for use.

5. Remove the cake from the oven and let it rest in the tin for 5 minutes. Drizzle with the 150–200ml (5–7fl oz) red wine, let it stand briefly, then remove from the tin and leave to cool on a wire rack.

6. When the cake is cold, pipe on the Chantilly cream and decorate with grape halves, grated white chocolate, and crushed almond brittle (if using).

▼

MARBLE CAKE

the classic version

For the cake: 300g (10oz) unsalted butter, at room temperature, plus extra for the tin • 350g (12oz) plain flour, plus extra for the tin • 75g (2½oz) icing sugar, plus extra for dusting • 7 eggs • seeds from ½ vanilla pod • finely grated zest of ½ unwaxed lemon • 2 drops of bitter almond extract • 100ml (3½fl oz) milk • 200g (7oz) caster sugar • 2 tsp baking powder • 25g (scant 1oz) cocoa powder
Equipment: 22cm (8½in) bundt tin • piping bag with round nozzle (optional)

Serves 16   Prep: 20 mins + cooling   Baking time: 50–60 mins

1. Preheat the oven to 180°C (350°F/Gas 4). Butter the bundt tin and dust it with flour, knocking out any excess from the tin.

2. Whisk together the butter and icing sugar in a bowl using an electric hand whisk. Separate the eggs. Add the egg yolks one at a time to the butter and sugar mix, beating well between each addition. Stir in the vanilla seeds, lemon zest, bitter almond extract, and milk.

3. Beat the egg whites using the scrupulously cleaned electric hand whisk on a medium setting, gradually adding the caster sugar as you go. Fold the whisked egg whites into the butter mixture. Finally, combine the flour with the baking powder and carefully fold into the mix.

4. Put about two-thirds of the mixture into the tin. Sift the cocoa over the remaining mixture and fold it in until all the ingredients are once more smoothly combined. For a particularly pretty marble effect, put the cocoa cake mix into a piping bag fitted with a round nozzle and pipe it into the lighter mix or, alternatively, you can create a less distinctive marbling by simply spooning the cocoa mix into the lighter mixture. Finally, run a fork through the mixture so that the light and dark mixtures intermingle slightly.

5. Bake the cake on the bottom shelf of the preheated oven for 50–60 minutes. To check whether it is done, stick a skewer into the cake. If there is no cake mix clinging to the skewer when you pull it out, the cake is ready. Remove from the oven and let it stand in the tin for about 5 minutes. Then turn the cake over onto a wire rack and let it cool under the tin. Dust with icing sugar to serve.

Tip: mini bundts
Instead of a large cake you can also bake lots of little ones; nowadays special mini bundt tins can be found almost anywhere. Dusted with icing sugar or decorated in your preferred style, these are the perfect finger food for a picnic or buffet. Remember they will need less time to bake; use the skewer test as instructed to help tell when mini bundt cakes are ready.

▼

CHOCOLATE BUNDT CAKE

à la Christian

For the cake: unsalted butter, for the tin • 200g (7oz) plain flour, plus extra for the tin • 100g (3½oz) milk chocolate • 80g (2¾oz) cocoa powder • 2 tsp baking powder • 2 large eggs • 250g (9oz) caster sugar • 155ml (5fl oz) flavourless vegetable oil • 125g (4½oz) extra thick double cream • 120ml (4fl oz) milk • seeds from 1 vanilla pod • finely grated zest of 1 unwaxed lemon • pinch of salt
For the chocolate icing and decoration: 4 leaves of gelatine • 75g (2½oz) caster sugar • 25g (scant 1oz) cocoa powder • 50g (1¾oz) double cream • 2 tbsp cocoa beans, for decoration (optional) • tempered white chocolate shards, for decoration (see p218)
Equipment: 22cm (8½in) bundt tin • sugar thermometer

Serves 12   Prep: 40 mins + 1 hr drying + cooling   Baking time: 50–60 mins

1. Preheat the oven to 150°C (300°F/Gas 2). Butter the bundt tin and dust with flour, knocking out any excess from the tin.

2. For the cake, finely chop the chocolate and melt it in a heatproof bowl suspended over simmering water (don't let the bowl touch the water). Mix the flour, cocoa powder, and baking powder.

3. Mix the eggs and sugar in a high-sided beaker using a hand-held blender until they are creamy. Trickle in the oil in a thin stream, mixing all the time, until it has the consistency of mayonnaise. Transfer into a bowl.

4. Combine the flour mixture with the creamed mixture using a balloon whisk. Stir in the double cream followed by the milk, vanilla, lemon zest, and salt. Finally, fold in the melted chocolate.

5. Spoon the mixture into the tin, smooth the surface and bake on the middle shelf of the preheated oven for 50–60 minutes. Insert a skewer into the centre of the cake to check whether it is done. If no

cake mixture clings to the skewer when you pull it out, the cake is ready. Remove from the oven and let it stand in the tin for about 5 minutes. Then turn the cake over onto a wire rack and let it cool down under the tin.

6. Meanwhile, soak the gelatine in cold water for 10 minutes ready to make the icing. Put the sugar and cocoa powder into a saucepan with 120ml (4fl oz) of water and bring to the boil, then remove from the heat. Squeeze out the gelatine and dissolve it in the warmed cocoa liquid. Mix in the cream using a hand-held blender, taking care not to incorporate any air. Cover the surface immediately with cling film to prevent it from forming a skin and let it cool to 45°C (113°F, see tip), monitoring the temperature with a sugar thermometer.

7. If desired, toast the cocoa beans in an oven preheated to 190°C (375°F/Gas 5) for 5–7 minutes, leave to cool, then grind. Cover the cake with the icing, press the ground cocoa beans around the lower edge and decorate with the white chocolate shards. Leave to dry for around 1 hour.

Tip: pay attention to temperature
When icing the cake, take special care not to get the glaze too hot or it will be dull rather than beautifully shiny. If the icing is worked at the ideal temperature, it will completely cover the cake, effectively sealing it. This ensures the cake will stay moist for longer. If you prefer, you can use white or milk chocolate for the icing.

▼

BLUEBERRY MADEIRA CAKE

with muesli

For the cake: 250g (9oz) unsalted butter, at room temperature, plus extra for the tin • 275g (9½oz) plain flour, plus extra for the tin • 1 tsp baking powder • 200g (7oz) good-quality muesli, plus 4 tbsp, for decoration • 210g (7½oz) icing sugar, plus 6 tbsp for icing • seeds from ½ vanilla pod • 100g (3½oz) good-quality marzipan • 6 eggs • 250g (9oz) blueberries, fresh or thawed from frozen, plus 125g (4½oz) fresh blueberries, for decoration (optional)
Equipment: loaf tin, 25cm (10in) in length

Serves 8   Prep: 20 mins + cooling   Baking time: 55 mins

1. Preheat the oven to 190°C (375°F/Gas 5). Butter the loaf tin and dust it with flour, shaking out excess. Mix the flour, baking powder, and muesli.

2. Beat the butter with the icing sugar and the vanilla seeds, in a bowl using an electric hand whisk on a medium setting, for around 5 minutes until creamy. In a second bowl beat the marzipan with an electric hand whisk until smooth, adding the eggs one at a time until the ingredients are smoothly combined. Stir the marzipan mixture into the butter mixture, then briefly stir in the flour mixture to combine. Finally, fold in the blueberries.

3. Spoon the cake batter into the loaf tin and smooth it out. Bake on the middle shelf of the preheated oven for 10 minutes. Then use a knife to make a lengthways cut, about 1cm (½in) deep, down the centre of the loaf. Reduce the oven temperature to 160°C (325°F/Gas 3) and bake for 45 minutes. Remove from the oven and leave to cool in the tin.

4. For the decoration, sprinkle the 4 tbsp muesli with 2 tbsp of the icing sugar in a saucepan and let it caramelize over a medium heat. To make the icing, mix the remaining icing sugar in a bowl with 1 tbsp of water and stir until smooth. Spread the icing over the cake, sprinkle with the caramelized muesli, and decorate with blueberries (if using).

Tip: dusting baking tins
Instead of flour you can also dust baking tins with ground almonds, other nuts, or biscuit crumbs, as appropriate, for extra interest.

▼

LIME POUND CAKE

with ginger

For the cake: 200g (7oz) unsalted butter, at room temperature, plus extra for the tin • 260g (9¼oz) plain flour, plus extra for the tin • 3 limes, plus fine strips of lime zest, for decoration (optional) • 60g (2oz) fresh root ginger • 150g (5½oz) caster sugar • 100g (3½oz) light brown sugar • pinch of salt • 4 eggs • 2 tsp baking powder

For the icing: 1 lime • 250g (9oz) icing sugar

Equipment: loaf tin, 25cm (10in) in length

Serves 8   Prep: 30 mins + 2 hrs drying + cooling   Baking time: 70–80 mins

1. Preheat the oven to 170°C (340°F/Gas 3½). Butter the loaf tin and dust it with flour, shaking out any excess.

2. Wash and rub dry the limes. Finely grate the zest. Squeeze the juice and set aside. Peel and finely chop or grate the ginger.

3. Cream the butter in a high-sided bowl with both types of sugar, the salt, lime zest, and ginger, using an electric hand whisk set to a medium speed, until the mixture is light and fluffy. Stir in the eggs one at a time, beating well after each addition. Combine the flour and baking powder and fold this in.

4. Spoon into the tin and smooth out. Bake on the middle shelf of the hot oven for 70–80 minutes. If it is browning too much, cover with foil after 35–45 minutes. Remove from the oven and let it cool a little in the tin.

5. Bring the reserved lime juice to the boil in a saucepan and pour evenly over the still-warm cake. Let the cake cool completely in the tin.

6. Squeeze the lime for the icing and stir with the icing sugar and 3–4 tbsp water to make a smooth, thick icing, being careful not to add too much. Cover the cake with the icing and scatter with the strips of lime zest (if using). Leave the icing to dry and set for 1–2 hours.

Tip: leaving the cake to cool
I like to leave pound cakes to cool down inside the cake tin. That way none of the moisture in the hot cake evaporates and it stays nice and moist.

▼

RHUBARB CAKE

with meringue topping

For the cake: 150g (5½oz) unsalted butter, plus extra for the tin • 600g (1lb 5oz) rhubarb • 150g (5½oz) caster sugar
• seeds from 1 vanilla pod • finely grated zest of 1 unwaxed lemon • 150g (5½oz) plain flour • 75g (2½oz) cornflour
• 1½ tsp baking powder • 2 eggs, plus 3 egg yolks
For the meringue: 4 egg whites • pinch of salt • 165g (5¾oz) caster sugar
Equipment: 26cm (10½in) springform tin

Serves 12–16   Prep: 45 mins + cooling   Baking time: 25–30 mins

1. Preheat the oven to 180°C (350°F/Gas 4) and butter the springform tin.

2. To make the cake, chop off the tough ends of the rhubarb stalks and chop the rhubarb into small cubes. Beat the butter with the sugar, vanilla seeds, and lemon zest, until light and creamy. Combine the flour, cornflour, and baking powder in a bowl. Gradually beat the eggs and egg yolks into the butter mixture, beating well after each addition, then stir in the flour mixture. Finally fold in the rhubarb. Spoon into the tin and bake on the middle shelf of the oven for around 20 minutes. Leave to cool.

3. Increase the oven temperature to 200°C (400°F/Gas 6) for the meringue. Whisk the egg whites with the salt and 3 tbsp of cold water in a bowl, using an electric hand whisk on a medium setting, until they

are stiff, gradually adding the sugar as you go. Let the mixture rest for around 10 minutes, then use a palette knife to spread it over the cake and bake it on the top shelf of the oven for 5–10 minutes until it is light brown. Leave the cake to cool, then carefully remove from the tin.

Tip: allow for resting time
Leave the meringue mixture to rest for 10 minutes at room temperature until it has formed a thin skin. This makes it more stable and reduces the chance of it collapsing when you bake it.

▼

DRESDEN SUGAR CAKE

with crunchy topping

For the cake: 125ml (4fl oz) milk, plus extra if needed • 15g (½oz) fresh yeast • 25g (scant 1oz) caster sugar • 250g (9oz) plain flour, plus extra if needed • pinch of salt • 35g (1¼oz) unsalted butter, at room temperature, plus extra for the tin

For the sugar topping: 180g (6oz) unsalted butter • 2 eggs • 180g (6oz) caster sugar • 40g (1¼oz) plain flour

Equipment: 28cm (11in) springform tin

Serves 12   Prep: 30 mins + 50 mins resting + cooling   Baking time: 25 mins

1. Heat the milk until lukewarm. Crumble in the yeast and stir in the sugar until the yeast dissolves.

2. Knead the flour with the salt, butter, and yeast mixture in a bowl until you have a smooth, elastic dough which comes away from the sides of the bowl. If necessary, add a little more milk or flour. Cover with a clean tea towel and leave the dough to prove at room temperature for around 30 minutes.

3. Butter the tin and arrange the dough inside, shaping the edges as you do this. Leave to prove for around 20 minutes at room temperature until it has clearly increased in size.

4. Meanwhile, preheat the oven to 190°C (375°F/ Gas 5). To make the sugar topping, melt the butter in a saucepan over a low heat. Stir the eggs, sugar, and flour in a bowl, add the melted butter and stir everything until it is smooth.

5. Pour the sugar topping evenly over the proven dough. Bake on the lower shelf of the preheated oven for around 25 minutes until golden brown. If the topping browns before the dough has cooked through, cover the cake with foil. Remove from the oven and let it cool in the tin.

Tip: proving yeast dough
The actual time required for a yeast dough to clearly increase in size depends greatly on the ambient temperature. At a normal room temperature of around 20°C (68°F), it will take roughly 30 minutes. Naturally, if the room is colder, the dough will prove more slowly; if it is warmer, it will increase in size more quickly.

▼

APRICOT CAKE

with almonds and vanilla blancmange

For the blancmange: 3 egg yolks • 1 sachet of vanilla blancmange mix • 330ml (11fl oz) milk • 330g (11oz) double cream • seeds from 1 vanilla pod • 50g (1¾oz) caster sugar • finely grated zest of ¼ unwaxed lemon
For the cake: 150g (5½oz) unsalted butter • 100g (3½oz) plain flour • 1 tsp baking powder • 250g (9oz) caster sugar • 100g (3½oz) ground almonds • pinch of salt • 8 egg whites
For the crumble and apricots: 210g (7½oz) plain flour • 100g (3½oz) light brown sugar • 1 tsp vanilla powder • 120g (4¼oz) unsalted butter, chopped • 300g (10oz) apricots
Equipment: 30 × 20cm (12 × 8in) rectangular baking tin, or 28cm (11in) springform tin • piping bag with round nozzle

Serves 15   Prep: 1 hr + 12 hrs chilling   Baking time: 1 hr

1. One day in advance, prepare the blancmange by mixing the egg yolks with the blancmange mix in a bowl with a balloon whisk. Bring the milk to the boil in a saucepan with the cream, vanilla seeds, and sugar, stirring continuously. Gradually pour the boiling milk mixture over the egg yolk mixture, stirring all the time. Return the whole thing to the pan and briefly bring to the boil again, stirring continuously, and allow to thicken. Push the mixture through a sieve and stir in the lemon zest. Cover with cling film, leave to cool and refrigerate.

2. The following day, preheat the oven to 190°C (375°F/Gas 5) and line the base of the cake tin with baking parchment.

3. To make the cake, first melt the butter in a pan over a medium heat. Combine the flour in a bowl with the baking powder, sugar, almonds, and salt. Whisk in the butter using an electric hand whisk, then carefully beat in the egg whites. Spoon the mixture into the tin.

4. For the crumble, rub together the flour, sugar, vanilla, and butter with your fingertips until you have coarse crumbs. Pit the apricots and cut each into 8. Scatter these over the cake batter, then follow with the crumble, and bake on the middle shelf of the preheated oven for 25 minutes.

5. Meanwhile, stir the vanilla blancmange with the balloon whisk so it is smooth again and transfer it to a piping bag fitted with a round nozzle. After 25 minutes baking time, remove the cake from the oven, leaving the oven turned on. Pipe small amounts of the blancmange into the cake, then continue baking for a further 35 minutes.

Tip: baking with other fruits
When baking with other fruits with a high water content, such as apples or pears, dust the segments with some flour, otherwise the water oozes out during baking and makes the cake mushy.

▼

INTERNATIONAL CLASSICS

Do you speak pudding?

....

Has your baking already taken you on a
sweet globetrotting journey to far-flung
destinations? No? Then the recipes in this
chapter will make it easy for you to travel,
without even leaving your kitchen. Indulge
your tastebuds while you cook your way
from America to France, via Italy to Sweden.

▼

AMERICAN CHEESECAKE

with passion fruit

For the base: 150g (5½oz) unsalted butter, chopped, at room temperature • 150g (5½oz) light brown sugar
• pinch of salt • seeds from ½ vanilla pod • 300g (10oz) plain flour • 1 egg yolk
For the filling: 450g (1lb) full-fat cream cheese • 120g (4¼oz) soured cream • 120g (4¼oz) caster sugar • 3 eggs
• seeds from 1 vanilla pod • finely grated zest of ½ unwaxed lemon • pinch of salt
For the jelly and decoration: 3 leaves of gelatine • 200g (7oz) passion fruit purée, ideally with seeds (with 10% sugar,
see p219), or passion fruit nectar or juice • tempered white chocolate shards, for decoration (optional, see p218)
• coconut flakes, toasted, for decoration (optional)
Equipment: 18cm (7in) springform tin

Serves 8   Prep: 30 mins + 2 hrs chilling + cooling   Baking time: 45–50 mins

1. Preheat the oven to 190°C (375°F/Gas 5). Line the base of the tin with baking parchment.

2. To make the cheesecake base, mix the butter, sugar, salt, vanilla seeds, and flour in a bowl and use your fingertips to rub everything together into a rough crumble. Spread the crumble over the base of the tin and press down well, making sure that all areas are covered. Bake on the middle shelf of the preheated oven for around 10 minutes until golden brown. Remove, brush with the egg yolk, and bake for another 5 minutes. Remove from the oven and leave to cool in the tin. Meanwhile, reduce the oven temperature to 150°C (300°F/Gas 2).

3. For the filling, stir together the cream cheese with the soured cream, sugar, eggs, vanilla seeds, lemon zest, and salt in a high-sided bowl, using a hand-held blender to produce a smooth cream. Take care not to incorporate any air in the mix.

4. Spoon the filling onto the cooled base. Bake on the middle shelf of the oven for 30–35 minutes. The mix should still wobble slightly in the centre, like a jelly; it will become firmer as it cools down.

5. Let the cheesecake cool in the tin on a wire rack for at least 2 hours. Then cover and refrigerate while you prepare the passion fruit jelly.

6. To make the jelly, soak the gelatine in a bowl of cold water for 10 minutes. Heat the passion fruit purée in a saucepan over a low heat, squeeze out the gelatine and let it dissolve in the warm purée (don't let it get too hot). Carefully spread the passion fruit jelly over the chilled cheesecake. Cover and refrigerate once more for around 2 hours, so that the jelly can set. Keep it there until you are ready to serve. Decorate the edge of the cheesecake with white chocolate shards or toasted coconut flakes (if using).

Tip: Fresh passion fruit
You could also use fresh passion
fruits, including the seeds, for
this jelly. Depending on their
size, you will need 5–7 fruits
to make 200g (7oz) jelly. To
prepare them, halve the fruits
and scoop out the flesh with a
spoon. Simmer in a saucepan
with 20g (¾oz) caster sugar for
5–10 minutes, until the flesh is
no longer clinging to the seeds.

▼

COFFEE CHEESECAKE

New York style

Serves 8   Prep: 20 mins + 2 hrs chilling + 2 hrs cooling   Baking time: 45–50 mins

For the base: 150g (5½oz) unsalted butter, chopped, at room temperature, plus extra for the tin • 150g (5½oz) light brown sugar • pinch of salt • seeds from ½ vanilla pod • 300g (10oz) plain flour • 1 tbsp instant coffee • 1 egg yolk
For the caramel sauce: 250g (9oz) caster sugar • 200g (7oz) double cream • 25g (scant 1oz) unsalted butter
For the filling: 450g (1lb) full-fat cream cheese • 120g (4¼oz) soured cream • 120g (4¼oz) caster sugar • 3 eggs • seeds from 1 vanilla pod • finely grated zest of ½ unwaxed lemon • pinch of salt
For the jelly and decoration: 3 leaves of gelatine • 200ml (7fl oz) strong brewed coffee • 100g (3½oz) double cream, for decoration • 1 tsp icing sugar • chocolate drops, for decoration (optional)
Equipment: 22cm (8½in) springform tin

1. Preheat the oven to 190°C (375°F/Gas 5). Butter the base of the springform tin and line a baking tray with baking parchment.

2. To make the base, mix the butter with the sugar, salt, vanilla seeds, flour, and instant coffee, and use your fingertips to rub it into a rough crumble. Evenly spread one-third of this on the baking tray. Transfer the rest to the springform tin and press down well, taking care that all of the base is covered.

3. Bake the base on the middle shelf of the preheated oven for around 10 minutes until golden brown. Brush with a little of the egg yolk and bake for another 5 minutes. Remove from the oven and let the base cool down slightly. In a similar way, bake the crumble on the baking tray for around 10 minutes until golden brown, remove from the oven and leave to cool on the tray. Reduce the oven temperature to 150°C (300°F/Gas 2).

4. For the caramel sauce, let the sugar caramelize in a high-sided saucepan over a medium heat. Pour in the cream and simmer over a low heat until the pieces of caramel dissolve. Mix in the butter using a hand-held blender. Spread over the base, reserving a small amount for decoration. Leave to cool.

5. To make the filling, mix the cream cheese, soured cream, sugar, eggs, vanilla seeds, lemon zest, and salt in a bowl using the hand-held blender. Take care not to incorporate any air.

6. Pour the filling over the caramel sauce and smooth it out. Bake the cheesecake on the middle shelf of the oven for 30–35 minutes. The centre should still wobble slightly in the middle, like a jelly; it will firm up as it sets. Remove from the oven and let it cool in the tin on a wire rack for at least 2 hours at room temperature.

7. To make the coffee jelly, soak the gelatine in a bowl of cold water for 10 minutes. Heat the coffee in a small saucepan, squeeze out the gelatine and dissolve it in the warmed coffee (don't let it get too hot). Spread the jelly over the surface of the cheesecake. Cover and refrigerate for around 2 hours so that the jelly can set. Whip the cream until it is stiff, sprinkling in the icing sugar. Spread the cream around the sides of the cheesecake. To serve, scatter with the baked crumble, trickle over the caramel sauce and decorate with chocolate drops (if using).

Tip: professional baking with a cake ring
You can also bake cheesecake and tart bases in metal cake rings, rather than springform tins. They are available in individual sizes, or you can also buy rings that are adjustable in diameter. Before baking, first line the metal ring with baking parchment, wrapping it over the edges. Then repeat with aluminium foil. Place the prepared ring on a baking tray and continue with the recipe as instructed.

▼

GERMAN CHEESECAKE

the classic version

For the pastry: 180g (6oz) unsalted butter, chopped, plus extra for the tin • 115g (4oz) icing sugar
• 1 small egg, plus 1 egg yolk • 1 tsp vanilla powder • seeds from ½ vanilla pod • pinch of salt
• 300g (10oz) plain flour, plus extra for the tin and for dusting • 35g (1¼oz) ground almonds
For the cheesecake and decoration: 100g (3½oz) unsalted butter • 1kg (2lb 4oz) low-fat quark • 190g (6½oz) caster
sugar • 80g (2¾oz) plain flour • finely grated zest of 1 unwaxed lemon • seeds from 1 vanilla pod • pinch of salt
• 5 eggs • 190g (6½oz) buttermilk • 4 tbsp apricot jam • 50g (1¾oz) flaked almonds • icing sugar, for dusting
Equipment: 26cm (10½in) springform • baking beans, dried pulses, or raw rice

Serves 12   Prep: 45 mins + 2 hrs chilling + cooling   Baking time: 80–90 mins

1. To make the pastry, knead together the butter, icing sugar, 1 egg, vanilla powder, vanilla seeds, and salt, in the bowl of a mixer fitted with a dough hook. Add the flour and almonds and work everything swiftly to a smooth consistency. Shape the pastry into a ball, press it flat, wrap in cling film and refrigerate for at least 2 hours.

2. Preheat the oven to 190°C (375°F/Gas 5). Lightly butter the tin and dust with flour, knocking out any excess. Roll out the pastry on a lightly floured work surface, or between 2 sheets of cling film, into a circle 5mm (¼in) thick. Use it to line the tin, to cover the base and rise 5cm (2in) up the sides. Trim so it is level and prick the base all over with a fork.

3. Line the pastry with baking parchment and fill with baking beans to weigh it down. Bake blind on the middle shelf of the preheated oven for 15 minutes. Remove the beans and baking parchment. Brush the pastry with egg yolk and bake for another 5 minutes until the egg yolk dries, sealing the pastry.

4. Meanwhile, prepare the cheesecake mixture. To do this, melt the butter in a pan over a low heat. Mix together the quark, sugar, flour, lemon zest, vanilla seeds, and salt in a high-sided bowl using an electric hand whisk. Gradually add the eggs and buttermilk, mixing all the time. Stir in the melted butter.

5. Remove the pastry case from the oven and fill it with the cheesecake mix. Return it to the oven and cook for 60–70 minutes. Let it cool completely in the tin. Cover and refrigerate until ready to serve. Briefly bring the apricot jam to the boil, press it through a sieve, then brush sparingly over the sides of the cake. Carefully press on the almonds all around and dust the top with icing sugar.

▼

CHEESECAKE MUFFINS

with double chocolate

For the muffins: 20g (¾oz) unsalted butter, plus extra for the moulds • 50g (1¾oz) dark chocolate
(75% cocoa solids, see tip, right) • 125g (4½oz) plain flour • 2 tsp baking powder • 25g (scant 1oz) cocoa powder
• 90g (3oz) caster sugar • 1 tsp vanilla powder • 125ml (4fl oz) milk • 1 large egg • 100g (3½oz) Chocolate Sauce
(see p145), to serve • icing sugar, for dusting
For the cheesecake mixture: 250g (9oz) full-fat cream cheese • 30g (1oz) caster sugar • 1 egg
For the chocolate crumble: 100g (3½oz) plain flour • 20g (¾oz) cocoa powder • 40g (1¼oz) caster sugar
• 60g (2oz) unsalted butter, chopped, at room temperature
Equipment: 12-hole muffin tray • 12 paper muffin cases (optional)

Makes 12   Prep: 30 mins + cooling   Baking time: 30 mins

1. Preheat the oven to 190°C (375°F/Gas 5). Butter the muffin moulds, or insert a paper case into each.

2. To make the muffins, melt the butter in a saucepan over a low heat. Chop the dark chocolate into small pieces and melt it in a heatproof bowl suspended over simmering water (don't let the bowl touch the water). Mix the flour in a bowl with the baking powder, cocoa powder, sugar, and vanilla powder.

3. Stir the melted butter, milk, and egg in a bowl with a balloon whisk until smooth. Pour the milk and egg mix into the flour mixture and stir with the balloon whisk just long enough to ensure that all the ingredients are well combined. Finally, fold in the melted dark chocolate. Spoon the mixture evenly between the muffin tray moulds or cases.

4. To make the cheesecake cream, stir the cream cheese with the sugar and egg in a bowl until smooth and divide evenly between the muffins.

5. To make the chocolate crumble, rub all the ingredients together with your fingertips in a bowl. Scatter evenly over the muffins.

6. Bake on the middle shelf of the preheated oven for around 30 minutes. Remove from the oven and let the muffins cool in the tin. Take them out of the tin and decorate with chocolate sauce and icing sugar.

Tip: removing lumps in cocoa powder
Mix cocoa powder with a small amount of the liquid ingredients before folding it into the mixture. The same applies for green tea powder, when using.

Tip: the right chocolate
For these muffins it is best to use a strong, bitter, high cocoa solids chocolate (ideally from a single-origin, characterful cocoa bean). It should have 75% cocoa solids. A powerful chocolate which is rich in character helps to balance the sweetness of these muffins.

Tip: glazed doughnuts
If you want to glaze the doughnuts, just stir 200g (7oz) icing sugar with 1–2 tbsp lemon juice or raspberry juice until it has a spreadable consistency. Spread this over the doughnuts and leave to set.

▼

DOUGHNUTS

with jam filling

For the dough: **400g (14oz) plain flour, plus extra if needed and for dusting** • **200ml (7fl oz) milk, plus extra if needed** • **15g (½oz) fresh yeast** • **40g (1¼oz) caster sugar** • **¼ tsp salt** • **1 egg, plus 1 egg yolk** • **45g (1½oz) unsalted butter, at room temperature**
For frying and filling: **about 2 litres (3½ pints) flavourless vegetable oil** • **about 150g (5½oz) raspberry jam, or another flavour if you prefer** • **icing sugar, for coating (optional)**
Equipment: **kitchen thermometer (optional)** • **piping bag with filler nozzle, or medium round nozzle**

Makes 12   Prep: 30 mins + 80 mins resting + 40 mins frying

1. Put the flour in a large bowl and form a well in the centre. Heat the milk until it is lukewarm, add the crumbled yeast and sugar and stir until the yeast has dissolved. Pour the milk mixture into the well in the flour and stir it with the flour to create a paste. Cover with a clean tea towel and leave to prove at room temperature for around 20 minutes.

2. Knead the dough with the salt, egg, and egg yolk until you have a smooth, elastic dough, gradually working in the butter as you knead. If necessary add a touch more flour or milk. Cover and leave to prove at room temperature for around 30 minutes until it has significantly increased in size.

3. Dust a baking tray with flour. Knead the dough briefly once more and divide it into 12 pieces. Shape each into a ball and lay on the tray with a 2cm (¾in) gap between them, cover, and leave to prove for 20–30 minutes until clearly increased in size.

4. Heat the oil for frying in a deep pan until it reaches 160–170°C (320–338°F), if possible monitoring the temperature with a kitchen thermometer, or hold a wooden spoon handle in the oil: the oil is hot enough when tiny bubbles rise up it. Gradually fry the doughnuts, in batches, for around 6 minutes on each side, turning with a slotted spoon, until golden brown. When frying the first side, keep the pan lid on; after turning the doughnuts to cook the second side, leave the pan lid off. Lift the doughnuts out using a slotted spoon, drain them on kitchen paper, and leave to cool on a wire rack.

5. To fill the doughnuts, stir the jam until it is smooth and transfer it into a piping bag fitted with a filler nozzle, or a medium round nozzle. Pipe jam into each doughnut. Roll in icing sugar (if using).

▼

CRONUTS

with blackberries

For the dough and for frying: 500g (1lb 2oz) plain flour, plus extra for dusting • ½ tsp salt • 200ml (7fl oz) milk
• 70g (2¼oz) caster sugar • 30g (1oz) fresh yeast • 1 egg • 30g (1oz) unsalted butter, at room temperature
• 2 litres (3½ pints) flavourless vegetable oil, for frying • icing sugar, for dusting
For the beurrage: 400g (14oz) unsalted butter • 120g (4¼oz) plain flour
For the filling: 200ml (7fl oz) blackcurrant juice, plus extra to taste • 100ml (3½fl oz) sour cherry juice (see p218)
• 100ml (3½fl oz) cranberry juice • 7g (¼oz) agar agar (see p218) • 40g (1¼oz) each raspberry, strawberry, and
blackberry purée (with 10% sugar, see p219), or just purée from a single fruit variety • 1 tbsp crème de cassis
• lime juice, to taste • 200g (7oz) fresh berries
Equipment: 8cm (3in) round doughnut cutter; or 4cm (1½in) and 8cm (3in) round cutters
• kitchen thermometer (optional) • piping bag with filler nozzle, or medium round nozzle

Makes 10   Prep: 70 mins + 3 hrs resting + 40 mins frying + chilling

1. To make the cronuts, prepare a yeast dough and beurrage, (see p217), and leave to prove, or store in a cool place.

2. Meanwhile, make the berry filling. Put the currant, cherry, and cranberry juices into a saucepan with the agar agar, bring to the boil and bubble for around 2 minutes (for the precise cooking time, refer to the packet instructions). Leave to cool, then pour into a bowl and let it set in the refrigerator. Use a hand-held blender to process the berry jelly with the raspberry, strawberry, and blackberry purées, and the crème de cassis, in a high-sided beaker or bowl until you have a smooth mixture which you can pipe. If it is too firm, add a little more juice. Add lime and blackcurrant juices to taste, cover, and refrigerate.

3. Continue the next steps with the yeast dough and beurrage (see p217): roll them out, fold together (single and double folds), and store in a cold place. Roll out the dough to about 3–4mm (⅛in) thick and use the cutter or cutters to stamp out rings. Turn them over, cover, and refrigerate for 10 minutes.

4. Meanwhile, heat the oil for frying in a high-sided pan to 180°C (350°F), and keep the temperature stable. Use a thermometer, or hold a wooden spoon handle in the oil: the oil is hot enough when tiny bubbles rise up it. Cook the dough rings carefully, in batches, in the hot oil for 4 minutes on both sides until golden brown, turning with a slotted spoon. Remove with a slotted spoon, let them drain, and lay them on kitchen paper to blot off the oil.

5. To finish, use a piping bag fitted with a filler nozzle to squirt in the berry filling. Serve with fresh berries and dust with icing sugar. Or slice the cronuts into thirds horizontally, pipe some of the filling onto the lower and middle rings, using a piping bag fitted with a round nozzle, cover with berries, and put the rings back together. Dust with icing sugar.

Tip: glazing cronuts
If you like you can ice the filled
cronuts with glacé or fondant
icing (see p219), decorating
with a few fresh berries.

Tip: for those in a hurry
If you are in a rush, you don't need to leave the mascarpone cream to firm up in a bowl before use. Just spread the cream straight onto the cake once you have mixed it and let it firm up in situ. It will be a little lighter and less creamy.

▼

CARROT CAKE

with mascarpone cream

For the cake: **4 carrots, around 500g (1lb 2oz) in total** • **440g (15½oz) plain flour** • **1½ tsp baking powder** • **1 tsp bicarbonate of soda** • **1 tsp ground cinnamon** • **pinch of freshly grated nutmeg** • **300g (10oz) caster sugar** • **4 eggs** • **finely grated zest of 1 orange** • **pinch of salt** • **300ml (½ pint) flavourless vegetable oil** • **40g (1¼oz) walnuts, chopped, plus more for decoration**
For the mascarpone cream and decoration: **3 leaves of gelatine** • **250g (9oz) double cream** • **3½ tbsp almond syrup (such as from Monin)** • **500g (1lb 2oz) mascarpone** • **50g (1¾oz) caster sugar** • **decorative carrots made from marzipan (optional)** • **finely grated orange zest, for decoration** • **Caramel Sauce (see p43)** • **icing sugar, for dusting**
Equipment: **30 × 20cm (12 × 8in) rectangular dessert frame**

Serves 15   Prep: 30 mins + 4 hrs chilling + cooling   Baking time: 25–30 mins

1. Preheat the oven to 180°C (350°F/Gas 4) and place the dessert frame on a baking tray lined with baking parchment. Peel and finely grate the carrots for the cake. Combine the flour, baking powder, bicarbonate of soda, cinnamon, and nutmeg.

2. Beat the sugar in a bowl with the eggs, orange zest, and salt using an electric hand whisk on a medium setting for 3 minutes. Trickle in the oil in a thin stream, still beating, then fold in the grated carrots, the flour mixture, and the walnuts. Spoon the cake batter into the dessert frame and smooth it over. Bake on the middle shelf of the preheated oven for 25–30 minutes. Remove from the oven and let it cool on the tray, then release from the frame.

3. Meanwhile, soak the gelatine for the mascarpone cream in cold water for 10 minutes. Whip the cream in a bowl using an electric hand whisk on a medium setting until it is just holding its shape. Warm the almond syrup in a pan, squeeze out the gelatine and dissolve it in the warmed syrup. Stir the mascarpone and sugar together in a bowl. Stir around 2 tbsp of the mascarpone mix into the syrup mixture, then swiftly combine this with the remaining mascarpone cream. Finally, carefully fold in the cream. Transfer the whole thing to a bowl, cover and refrigerate to set for 2 hours.

4. Stir up the mascarpone cream with a balloon whisk. Cut the carrot sponge horizontally into 3 pieces and spread the base section with cream. Lay the second section on top and cover with cream. Put the third piece on top, spread it with cream and refrigerate the cake for a further 2 hours. Decorate with marzipan carrots (if using), walnuts, grated orange zest, caramel sauce, and icing sugar.

▼

HOME-MADE MARSHMALLOWS

with chocolate

For the marshmallows: cocoa powder, for dusting • 8 leaves of gelatine • 170g (5¾oz) liquid glucose
• 125g (4½oz) dark chocolate (70% cocoa solids) • 225g (8oz) caster sugar • 75ml (2½fl oz) carbonated mineral water
Equipment: 40 × 15cm (16 × 6in) rectangular tin (such as a roasting tin) • sugar thermometer or kitchen thermometer

Makes about 65   Prep: 30 mins + 12 hrs chilling

1. Dampen the tin with some water and line with cling film. Put some cocoa powder into a small fine sieve and use it to dust the tin all over.

2. Soak the gelatine in cold water for 10 minutes. Put 140g (5oz) of the liquid glucose in the bowl of a food processor fitted with a balloon whisk. Chop the chocolate and melt it in a heatproof bowl over simmering water (don't let it touch the water).

3. Heat the sugar in a saucepan with the remaining liquid glucose and the mineral water to 110°C (230°F), stirring continuously and monitoring the temperature with a thermometer. Switch the food processor on at a medium speed and slowly pour in the hot sugar syrup, in a thin stream.

4. Squeeze out the gelatine thoroughly and add to the food processor while it is still running. Then continue to beat on a medium-high setting until the bowl has cooled so that it is almost warm to the touch (about 40°C/104°F).

5. Switch the food processor to a medium speed and slowly pour the melted chocolate into the mixture. Turn off the machine, stir in any dregs using a spatula, then beat the mixture briefly once more on a medium setting.

6. Transfer the marshmallow mixture into the tin, dust with more sifted cocoa powder, cover with cling film so that it is airtight and refrigerate to let it solidify for around 12 hours. Cut into 3–4cm (1¼–1½in) large cubes and dust with cocoa powder.

▼

STRAWBERRY MARSHMALLOWS

with a hint of lemon

For the marshmallows: **dextrose, for dusting (see p218)** • **7 leaves of gelatine** • **1 unwaxed lemon** • **225g (8oz) caster sugar** • **170g (5¾oz) isomalt (invert sugar, see p218)** • **125g (4½oz) cocoa butter** • **50g (1¾oz) strawberry purée (with 10% sugar, see p219)**
Equipment: 30 × 20cm (12 × 8in) rectangular tin (such as a roasting tin) • sugar thermometer or kitchen thermometer (see tip)

Makes about 50   Prep: 30 mins + 5 hrs chilling

1. Dampen the tin with some water and line with cling film. Put some dextrose into a small fine sieve and use it to dust the tin all over.

2. Soak the gelatine in cold water for 10 minutes. Wash the lemon in hot water and rub it dry. Finely grate the zest and squeeze out the juice.

3. Heat the caster sugar with 2 tsp of the lemon juice (save the rest for another recipe), 2 tbsp of water and 70g (2¼oz) of the isomalt in a saucepan over a medium heat to 110°C (230°F), stirring continuously and monitoring with a thermometer.

4. Mix the remaining isomalt with the sugar syrup and lemon zest in a large metal bowl. Squeeze out the gelatine and stir it in. Beat until the mixture is lukewarm, then add the cocoa butter and strawberry purée. Beat until the mixture reaches 35–40°C (95–104°F), then transfer into the prepared tin.

5. Dust the marshmallow mixture with more dextrose, cover with cling film so that it is airtight, and refrigerate to set for around 12 hours. Cut into 3–4cm (1¼–1½in) large cubes and, if you like, dust the cut surfaces with dextrose.

Tip: it won't work without a thermometer
To achieve the perfect marshmallow consistency, it is important to use a thermometer that can withstand high temperatures and which is accurate to the nearest degree. The best thing to use is a special sugar thermometer, but an accurate digital kitchen thermometer for temperatures up to 200°C (400°F) can also be used.

▼

PEANUT BUTTER BROWNIES

with caramel sauce

For the brownies: 150g (5½oz) unsalted peanuts • 2 tbsp icing sugar • 400g (14oz) dark chocolate • 300g (10oz) unsalted butter • 12 eggs • 45g (1½oz) caster sugar • 400g (14oz) light brown sugar • 3½ tbsp hazelnut oil, or flavourless vegetable oil • 150g (5½oz) plain flour • 60g (2oz) cocoa powder • 300g (10oz) peanut butter, for decoration • chocolate flakes
For the caramel sauce: 300g (10oz) caster sugar • 300g (10oz) double cream • 30g (1oz) unsalted butter
Equipment: 40 × 30cm (16 × 12in) deep baking tray • piping bag with medium round nozzle (optional)

Makes 20   Prep: 30 mins + cooling   Baking time: 25–30 mins

1. Preheat the oven to 200°C (400°F/Gas 6) and line the baking tray with baking parchment. Spread the peanuts out on another baking tray, dust with the icing sugar, and let them caramelize on the middle shelf of the preheated oven for 5–10 minutes. Leave to cool, then roughly chop. Set aside 50g (1¾oz) of the chopped peanuts for decoration. Finely chop the chocolate and melt it with the butter in a heatproof bowl over simmering water (don't let the bowl touch the water), stirring occasionally as it melts.

2. Beat the eggs with the caster sugar and light brown sugar in a bowl using an electric hand whisk until thick and creamy. Stir the hazelnut oil into the melted chocolate mixture, then gradually beat this into the egg and sugar mix. Sift the flour and cocoa powder together and fold in. Finally, carefully fold in the caramelized peanuts.

3. Spoon the batter evenly over the baking tray and bake on the middle shelf of the preheated oven for around 20 minutes until a crisp layer of caramelized sugar is visible on the surface. Remove from the oven, let the brownie cool on the tray and cut into 20 equal-sized pieces.

4. To make the caramel sauce, let the sugar caramelize in a saucepan over a medium heat. Pour in the cream and continue to simmer over a low heat until the caramel dissolves. Finally, work in the butter using a hand-held blender, to give a smooth sauce. Cover and refrigerate until ready to use.

5. To decorate, if you like, you can fill a piping bag fitted with a round nozzle with the peanut butter and pipe this onto the brownies, or just dollop it on in blobs with a spoon. Drizzle caramel sauce over the peanut butter and scatter with chocolate flakes and the reserved caramelized peanuts.

▼

EXQUISITE MADELEINES

A French classic

For the cakes: **65g (2¼oz) plain flour** • **1 tsp baking powder** • **pinch of salt** • **75g (2½oz) unsalted butter** • **2 eggs, plus 1 egg yolk** • **75g (2½oz) caster sugar** • **seeds from ½ vanilla pod**
Equipment: 1–2 × 20-hole silicone madeleine baking moulds (each hole 4 × 3cm / 1½ × 1¼in)
• piping bag with medium round nozzle

Makes about 40   Prep: 20 mins + 12 hrs resting + cooling   Baking time: 15 mins

1. Mix the flour, baking powder, and salt. Melt the butter in a saucepan over a low heat. Beat the eggs with the egg yolk, sugar, and vanilla seeds in a bowl using an electric hand whisk until light and creamy.

2. Fold the flour mixture into the egg mixture just enough to produce a smooth consistency. Slowly stir in the melted butter and mix until everything is smooth. Cover and refrigerate to let the mixture rest for 12 hours.

3. Preheat the oven to 210°C (410°F/Gas 6½). Transfer the mixture into a piping bag fitted with a round nozzle and pipe into the madeleine moulds so that each is two-thirds full. If you only have a single silicone tray, leave half the mixture in the refrigerator and bake the madeleines in 2 batches.

4. Bake the madeleines on the middle shelf of the preheated oven for 2–3 minutes until the edges rise up slightly. Switch off the oven, but do not open it. After a further 2–3 minutes the centre of the madeleines will swell up into a domed shape. Turn the oven back on to the reduced temperature of 190°C (375°F/Gas 5) and finish baking the madeleines for around 10 minutes until golden brown. Pop out of the mould or moulds and leave to cool on a wire rack.

Tip: lemon madeleines
To make a refreshing, fruity version, wash an unwaxed lemon and dry it well. Finely grate the zest and stir into the madeleine batter. Bake the madeleines as instructed.

▼

FINANCIERS

with vanilla blancmange

For the blancmange: **125ml (4fl oz)** milk • **125g (4½oz)** double cream • seeds from ½ vanilla pod
• **40g (1¼oz)** caster sugar • **3** egg yolks • **10g (¼oz)** vanilla blancmange mix
For the cakes: **150g (5½oz)** unsalted butter • **100g (3½oz)** plain flour • **1 tsp** baking powder • **250g (9oz)** caster sugar
• **100g (3½oz)** ground almonds • pinch of salt • **250g (9oz)** egg white (from about 7 eggs)
• fresh fruits, for decoration (such as raspberries or blackberries) • icing sugar, for dusting
Equipment: piping bag with medium round nozzle
• 12-hole silicone mini-loaf baking mould (each hole 8 × 3cm / 3 × 1¼in)

Makes 12   Prep: 30 mins + 1 hr chilling + cooling   Baking time: 25 mins

1. For the vanilla blancmange, bring the milk, cream, vanilla seeds, and sugar to the boil in a saucepan. Meanwhile, beat the egg yolks with the blancmange mix in a bowl using a balloon whisk. Gradually pour in the milk mixture, beating continuously. Return it to the saucepan and let it simmer and thicken for a further minute, stirring all the time. Remove from the hob and continue to stir so that the egg yolk doesn't curdle in the hot mixture. Strain through a fine sieve, cover, and allow to cool slightly at room temperature. Now lay cling film directly on the surface to prevent a skin from forming and refrigerate for about 1 hour.

2. Make the financiers. Preheat the oven to 190°C (375°F/Gas 5). Melt the butter in a saucepan over a medium heat. Mix the flour with the baking powder, sugar, ground almonds, and salt in a bowl. Firstly beat in the butter using an electric hand whisk, then beat in the egg whites.

3. Spoon the mixture into a piping bag fitted with a round nozzle. Pipe into the holes of the mould until each is two-thirds full. Bake the financiers on the middle shelf of the oven for around 12 minutes. Meanwhile, transfer around one-third of the cold blancmange into the cleaned piping bag fitted with a round nozzle. Remove the baking tray from the oven and pipe 3 blobs of blancmange into each financier so that just a little peeps out.

4. Finish baking the financiers in the oven for around 12 minutes until golden brown. Remove from the oven and leave to cool in the mould. Then pop them out of the mould and decorate with the remaining vanilla blancmange and some fruit (if using), before dusting with icing sugar.

Tip: be flexible
Vary the basic financiers mix every now and again by stirring in citrus fruit zests: try orange, lime, or lemon. If you also add a dash of the relevant juice, the result will be particularly light. Fill citrus financiers with chocolate blancmange instead of vanilla, or simply tuck a couple of pieces of chocolate into the half-baked mix.

▼

ÉCLAIRS

with strawberries and mascarpone

For the choux pastry: **125ml (4fl oz) milk** • **pinch of salt** • **1 tbsp caster sugar** • **120g (4¼oz) unsalted butter**
• **150g (5½oz) plain flour** • **4 eggs**
For the mascarpone cream and decoration: **3 leaves of gelatine** • **250g (9oz) double cream**
• **500g (1lb 2oz) mascarpone** • **50g (1¾oz) caster sugar** • **50g (1¾oz) almond syrup (such as sold by Monin)**
• **500g (1lb 2oz) strawberries** • **icing sugar, for dusting**
Equipment: **piping bag with large round nozzle**

Makes about 20   Prep: 30 mins + 1 hr chilling + cooling   Baking time: 40 mins

The French word éclair translates as 'lightning', perhaps because the whole thing will be devoured
at lightning speed…

1. Preheat the oven to 180°C (350°F/Gas 4) and line a baking tray with baking parchment.

2. To make the choux pastry, put the milk in a saucepan with 125ml (4fl oz) of water, the salt, sugar, and butter and bring to the boil. Remove the saucepan from the hob, add the flour all at once and stir together. Return the pan to the heat and dry out the dough for around 1 minute: stir it over the heat until it clumps into a ball and a white residue has formed on the base of the saucepan.

3. Transfer the dough to a bowl. Whisk the eggs with a fork and gradually add to the still-warm dough, beating with an electric hand whisk on a low setting until a smooth, shiny consistency is achieved.

4. Spoon into a piping bag fitted with a round nozzle and pipe 10cm (4in) long, 2cm (¾in) wide strips onto the tray. Bake on the middle shelf of the oven for 40 minutes until golden brown all over. Do not open the oven or take the éclairs out too soon or the dough will collapse. Cool on a wire rack.

5. To make the mascarpone cream, soak the gelatine in cold water for 10 minutes. Meanwhile, use an electric hand whisk to whip the cream in a bowl until it is just holding its shape. Stir the mascarpone together with the sugar in a bowl. Gently heat the almond syrup in a saucepan, squeeze out the gelatine and dissolve it in the almond syrup. Stir around 2 tbsp of the mascarpone mix into the almond syrup mixture, then swiftly fold this into the remaining mascarpone mix, taking care that you don't get any lumps of gelatine. Finally, carefully fold in the cream. Cover and refrigerate to firm up for 1 hour.

6. Meanwhile, halve or quarter the strawberries depending on their size. To serve, split the éclairs in half horizontally. Stir the mascarpone cream until it is smooth using a balloon whisk, spoon into the cleaned piping bag fitted with a round nozzle and pipe dots onto the lower half of the éclairs. Arrange the strawberries in between the cream. Replace the upper half of each éclair and dust with icing sugar.

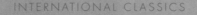

▼

ÉCLAIRS

with chocolate orange cream

Makes about 20   Prep: 30 mins + 24 hrs chilling + cooling   Baking time: 40 mins

For the chocolate orange cream and decoration: 180g (6oz) dark chocolate (60% cocoa solids), plus 200g (7oz) for decoration • 30g (1oz) unsalted butter • 2½ tbsp orange juice • 200g (7oz) double cream • finely grated zest of 1 orange, plus extra for decoration (optional) • 20g (¾oz) liquid glucose • orange segments, for decoration
For the choux pastry: 125ml (4fl oz) milk • pinch of salt • 1 tbsp caster sugar • 120g (4¼oz) unsalted butter • 150g (5½oz) plain flour • 4 eggs
Equipment: piping bag with large round nozzle • piping bag with small round nozzle

1. One day in advance, finely chop the 180g (6oz) of chocolate for the chocolate and orange cream. Melt the butter in a heatproof bowl over simmering water. Remove the bowl from the water, stir in the chocolate and allow it to melt.

2. Bring the orange juice to the boil in a saucepan with 175g (6oz) of the cream, the orange zest, and liquid glucose. Pour the hot juice mixture over the chocolate mix and let it stand for 2 minutes. Stir together using a hand-held blender or spatula, taking care not to incorporate any air. Gradually stir in the remaining cream. Cover and refrigerate for at least 24 hours.

3. The following day, when ready to bake, preheat the oven to 180°C (350°F/Gas 4) and line a baking tray with baking parchment.

4. To make the choux pastry, bring the milk to the boil in a saucepan with 125ml (4fl oz) of water, the salt, sugar, and butter and bring to the boil. Remove the pan from the hob, add the flour all at once and stir together. Return the saucepan to the heat and dry out the dough for around 1 minute: stir it over the heat until it clumps into a ball and a white residue has formed on the base of the saucepan

5. Transfer the dough to a bowl. Whisk the eggs with a fork and gradually add to the still-warm dough, beating with an electric hand whisk on a low setting until a smooth, shiny consistency is achieved.

6. Spoon into a piping bag fitted with a large round nozzle and pipe 10cm (4in) long, 2cm (¾in) wide strips onto the baking tray. Bake on the middle shelf of the preheated oven for 40 minutes until they are golden brown all over. Do not open the oven or take the éclairs out too soon or the dough will collapse. Let cool on a wire rack.

7. Split the éclairs in half horizontally. Finely chop the remaining 200g (7oz) of dark chocolate and let it melt in a heatproof bowl placed over simmering water (don't let the bowl touch the water). Cover the upper half of the éclairs with the chocolate and leave to set.

8. To serve, beat the chocolate orange cream just briefly with an electric hand whisk on a medium setting until the mixture is firm and smooth. Spoon the cream into a piping bag fitted with a small round nozzle and pipe dots onto the lower half of the éclairs. Insert orange segments in between. Replace the upper section of the éclairs and decorate with orange zest (if using).

Tip: white chocolate writing
In the baking section of most supermarkets nowadays you will find little tubes of white chocolate which you can pipe on for decoration. These can be used for additional decoration of the chocolate covered éclairs, if you like.

▼

RUM BABAS

juicy and delicious

For the dough: 400g (14oz) plain flour • 130g (4½oz) unsalted butter, at room temperature • 25g (scant 1oz) honey • 15g (½oz) fresh yeast • ½ tsp salt • 10 eggs
For the syrup: 250g (9oz) caster sugar • seeds from 1 vanilla pod • finely grated zest of 1 unwaxed lemon • finely grated zest of 1 orange • 120ml (4fl oz) dark rum, or to taste
For the cream: 400g (14oz) double cream • 80g (2¾oz) caster sugar • seeds from ½ vanilla pod
Equipment: 2 × 8-hole silicone savarin baking moulds (each hole 4.5cm / 1¾in in diameter)

Makes 12–16   Prep: 30 mins + 40 mins resting + cooling   Baking time: 25–30 mins

1. To make the dough, mix together the flour, butter, honey, crumbled yeast, and salt in the bowl of a mixer fitted with the dough hook attachment. Gradually add the eggs and knead until you have a smooth dough which comes away from the sides of the bowl. Leave to rest at room temperature for 10 minutes, covered with a clean tea towel.

2. Half-fill each of the silicone moulds with the dough, cover and leave to prove at room temperature for around 30 minutes, until the mix reaches the rim of the moulds. Meanwhile, preheat the oven to 210°C (410°F/Gas 6½). Cook the babas on the middle shelf of the preheated oven for 25–30 minutes until they are golden brown.

3. Meanwhile, prepare the syrup. In a saucepan, stir together 500ml (18fl oz) of water with the sugar, vanilla seeds, and lemon and orange zests and bring to the boil, stirring until the sugar dissolves. Remove from the heat and add rum to taste.

4. Place a wire rack on a baking tray or in a large casserole dish. Remove the silicone mould from the oven, pop out the babas one at a time and use a slotted spoon to dip them into the no-longer boiling syrup, soaking each individually. Leave to drain and cool on the wire rack.

5. To serve, put the cream in a bowl with the sugar and vanilla seeds and use an electric hand whisk on a medium setting to whip it until just holding its shape. Serve the babas with the whipped cream.

Tip: experiment a little
You must be careful not to dip the babas in the liquid for too long or they can easily become mushy, but by all means vary the soaking time according to taste. Some people prefer them rather crisper, others favour a softer texture. You can also experiment with the alcohol; a more summery creation can be conjured up by using a mojito instead of rum.

▼

CHELSEA BUNS

with a nut filling

For the dough: 500g (1lb 2oz) plain flour, plus extra if needed and for dusting • 200–250ml (7–9fl oz) milk, plus extra if needed • 45g (1½oz) caster sugar • 25g (scant 1oz) fresh yeast • 1 egg • 100g (3½oz) unsalted butter, at room temperature, plus extra for the cake ring and for brushing
For the crème pâtissière: 80g (2¾oz) caster sugar • 3 egg yolks • 1 heaped tbsp vanilla blancmange mix • 330ml (11fl oz) milk • ½ vanilla pod
For the filling: 200g (7oz) chopped hazelnuts • 100g (3½oz) ground hazelnuts • 150g (5½oz) caster sugar • 1 egg • 2 tbsp rum • 4 tbsp milk
Equipment: 28cm (11in) cake ring

Makes 8–10   Prep: 30 mins + 80 mins resting + cooling   Baking time: 70 mins

1. To make the yeast dough, put the flour in a large bowl and make a well in the centre. Heat the milk until it is lukewarm. Stir the sugar and crumbled yeast together with the milk until the yeast has dissolved. Stir the milk mixture into the well in the flour and mix in the flour. Cover with a clean tea towel and leave to prove for around 20 minutes.

2. Add the egg and knead everything for 5–10 minutes until you have a smooth, elastic dough. Gradually work in the butter as you knead. If necessary, add a touch more milk or flour. Leave the yeasted dough to prove for around 30 minutes until it has doubled in volume.

3. To make the crème pâtissière, stir together 1 tbsp of the sugar with the egg yolks and blancmange powder in a bowl. Put the milk in a saucepan with the vanilla pod, the scraped-out vanilla seeds, and the remaining sugar and bring to the boil, stirring constantly. Remove the vanilla pod and pour the boiling milk into the egg yolk mixture, stirring vigorously all the time. Return to the saucepan and bring it briefly to the boil again, stirring all the time.

Finally, decant immediately into a cold bowl, cover the surface with cling film to prevent a skin from forming, and leave to cool.

4. Stir together all the ingredients for the filling. Line a baking tray with baking parchment. Butter the cake ring and place it on the tray. Knead the dough briefly once again and roll it out on a lightly floured work surface to a 40 × 30cm (16 × 12in) rectangle. Spread with the crème pâtissière and the nut filling and roll it up tightly from the long side. Cut into about 4–5cm (1½–2in) slices. Place these next to one another in the cake ring, cut sides facing up. Leave to prove again for around 30 minutes.

5. Preheat the oven to 180°C (350°F/Gas 4). Melt some butter for brushing. Brush the buns with the butter and bake on the middle shelf of the preheated oven for 70 minutes until golden brown. Remove from the oven and leave to cool on a wire rack.

▼

PIEDMONT HAZELNUT TART

with marzipan sponge and Baileys ganache

For the pastry: 150g (5½oz) unsalted butter, chopped, plus extra for the tins • 100g (3½oz) icing sugar
• 30g (1oz) ground hazelnuts • 1 egg • 250g (9oz) plain flour
For the nougat filling: 400g (14oz) caster sugar • 330g (11oz) hazelnut nougat • 35g (1¼oz) ground hazelnuts
For the sponge: 65g (1¼oz) dark chocolate • 50g (1¾oz) unsalted butter • 200g (7oz) good-quality marzipan
• 115g (4oz) caster sugar • 1 large egg, plus 5 medium egg yolks, plus 4 medium egg whites
• 70g (2¼oz) plain flour
For the Baileys ganache: 80g (2¾oz) extra thick double cream • 25g (scant 1oz) liquid glucose (see p219)
• 10g (¼oz) honey • 280g (9½oz) milk chocolate, finely chopped • 1½ tbsp Baileys liqueur
For the Chantilly cream and decoration: 200g (7oz) ground hazelnuts • 100g (3½oz) extra thick or regular double
cream • 25g (scant 1oz) caster sugar • seeds from ½ vanilla pod • 100g (3½oz) caramelized nuts (optional, see p43)
Equipment: 3 × 26cm (16¼in) springform tins • baking beans, dried pulses, or raw rice • sugar thermometer

Serves 12   Prep: 40 mins + 5½ hrs chilling + cooling   Baking time: 35–40 mins

1. To make the pastry, rub the butter and icing sugar together by hand or using a mixer fitted with a dough hook. Next knead in the hazelnuts, then the egg. Sift in the flour and quickly work to a smooth consistency. Shape into a ball, press flat, wrap in cling film, and refrigerate for at least 2 hours.

2. Preheat the oven to 180°C (350°F/Gas 4) with the fan on and butter the springform tin. Roll out the pastry to a 5mm- (¼in-) thick disc the size of the base of the tin and bake blind for 30 minutes, lined with baking parchment and baking beans (see p59). Leave in the tin. Any leftover pastry freezes well.

3. For the filling, butter a baking tray and warm it in an oven set to 100°C (212°F/Gas ¼). Let the sugar lightly caramelize in a saucepan over a medium heat. Melt the nougat to 80°C (176°F) in a heatproof bowl over simmering water. Take the tray from the oven and pour on the sugar, then the melted nougat.

4. Toss the sugar and nougat with 2 spatulas, turning repeatedly so you get several layers of sugar and nougat. Spread half the nuts and half the sugar-nougat mixture over the shortcrust base. Line another springform tin with baking parchment, scatter over the remaining nuts, and pour in the rest of the sugar-nougat mixture. Cover both and refrigerate for around 30 minutes to set.

5. Preheat the oven to 200°C (400°F/Gas 6). Finely chop the chocolate for the sponge and melt it with the butter in a heatproof bowl placed over simmering water (don't let the bowl touch the water). Mix the marzipan with 50g (1¾oz) of the sugar in a bowl using an electric hand whisk, until completely smooth. Beat the egg with the egg yolks and gradually stir into the marzipan mixture, whisking for 5 minutes until everything is creamy. Add the chocolate mixture and beat for a further 5 minutes until the batter is thick and creamy.

6. Whisk the egg whites until they are stiff, gradually adding the remaining sugar as you do so. Fold the whisked egg whites into the marzipan mixture. Sift over the flour and fold it in. Spread the batter in a third springform lined with baking paper so it is around 1cm (½in) thick and bake on the middle shelf of the preheated oven for 7 minutes. Leave to cool, split in half horizontally and freeze the second disc for later use.

7. To make the ganache, bring the cream to the boil with the glucose and honey. Pour this over the chocolate and mix with a hand-held blender, taking care not to incorporate any air. Mix in the Baileys.

8. Lay the chocolate sponge on the shortcrust base with nougat filling, place the second nougat disc on top and spread with the ganache. Finally, decorate by scattering with the 200g (7oz) ground hazelnuts and freeze for 3 hours.

9. Make the Chantilly cream by whisking the cream with the sugar and vanilla seeds. Before serving, carefully release the tart from the springform, spread the edge and sides of the tart with the Chantilly cream and decorate with caramelized nuts (if using).

Tip: cake rings instead of springforms
Instead of springform tins you can also use metal cake rings (see p83) to bake pastry bases, or indeed use a combination of both for multi-stage recipes such as this.

▼

TARTE TATIN

with apples or figs

For the tarte: 3 tart apples, about 450g (1lb) in total, or 450g (1lb) fresh figs • 100g (3½oz) unsalted butter • 100g (3½oz) caster sugar • 275g (9½oz) ready-rolled puff pastry sheet
Equipment: 20–22cm (8–9in) ovenproof cast-iron frying pan

Serves 8   Prep: 20 mins + cooling   Baking time: 30 mins

1. Peel, quarter and core the apples. Cut the apples into slices roughly 1cm (½in) thick. Alternatively, quarter the figs or cut them lengthways into slices.

2. Let the butter and sugar caramelize lightly in a cast-iron frying pan over a medium heat. Remove the pan from the hob and let the butter and sugar mixture cool down slightly.

3. Meanwhile, preheat the oven to 220°C (425°F/Gas 7) with the fan on. Lay the apple or fig slices on the caramel in the pan to form a fan shape, so the base of the pan is completely covered.

4. Cut out the puff pastry sheet into a circle about 1cm (½in) bigger than the base of the frying pan. Lay it on top of the apples or figs and press down lightly around the edges of the fruit. Bake the tarte tatin on the middle shelf of the preheated oven for around 30 minutes until golden brown, cracking the oven door open slightly after 10 minutes so any moisture can escape.

5. Remove the pan from the oven and place a plate of the same diameter as the pan on top of the tart. Wearing heatproof gloves, flip over the pan together with the plate as quickly as possible. When doing this, take care that the plate is pressed firmly onto the rim of the pan so that no liquid can escape. Remove the pan from the flipped-over tart and carefully rearrange the fruit, if necessary. Serve lukewarm or completely cold.

Tip: use puff pastry remnants as decoration
You can make wonderfully effective decorations for the tart from the puff pastry remnants. To do this, place the puff pastry remnants on a baking tray, brush them with a bit of melted butter and dust with icing sugar. Once the tart is cooked, put the tray on the middle shelf of the oven and bake until golden brown. Remove from the oven and leave to cool on a wire rack. Pick the caramelized pastry sheet into pieces by hand and use to decorate the tart.

▼

ORANGE CAKE

with polenta

For the cake: 60g (2oz) plain flour • 160g (5¾oz) fine polenta • 2 tsp baking powder • 1–2 oranges, plus 4 oranges
for topping, plus fine strips of orange zest, for decoration • 310g (10¼oz) unsalted butter, at room temperature
• 210g (7½oz) caster sugar • 5 eggs • 75g (2½oz) plain yogurt • 4 tbsp apricot jam
Equipment: 40 × 30cm (16 × 12in) baking tray

Serves 15   Prep: 30 mins + cooling   Baking time: 20 mins

1. Preheat the oven to 180°C (350°F/Gas 4) and line a baking tray with baking parchment. Mix together the flour, polenta, and baking powder. Wash the 1–2 oranges under hot water, dry, and finely grate the zest. Halve the oranges, squeeze them and measure out 125ml (4fl oz) of the juice (see tip, right).

2. Cream the butter and sugar in a bowl using an electric hand whisk. Add the eggs one at a time, beating well after each addition. Then beat in the yogurt on a low setting before adding the orange zest and the measured-out orange juice. Finally, fold the flour and polenta mixture.

3. Spread the batter over the baking tray and smooth it out. Let it stand for around 10 minutes so the polenta can swell. Bake on the middle shelf of the preheated oven for 20 minutes until golden brown.

4. Remove the cake from the oven and let it cool on the baking tray. Grate over most of the zest of 1 of the remaining oranges, then cut all 4 oranges into segments, removing any bitter white pith. Warm the jam in a saucepan, then press it through a sieve, stirring in a bit of the orange zest. Decorate the cake with the orange segments, brush with the warm jam glaze, and scatter with the remaining orange zest.

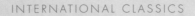

▼

MILANESE CHERRY TARTLETS

with mascarpone

Makes 6   Prep: 1 hr + 1 hr chilling + cooling   Baking time: 30 mins

For the dacquoise sponge: 150g (5½oz) egg whites (from about 4 eggs) • pinch of salt • 150g (5½oz) caster sugar • 150g (5½oz) icing sugar • 120g (4¼oz) ground almonds • 30g (1oz) plain flour
For the chocolate crumble: 50g (1¾oz) unsalted butter, chopped • 25g (scant 1oz) plain flour • 20g (¾oz) cocoa powder • 50g (1¾oz) light brown sugar • seeds from 1 vanilla pod • icing sugar, for dusting
For the mascarpone cream: 2 leaves of gelatine • 170g (5¾oz) double cream • 330g (11oz) mascarpone • 30g (1oz) caster sugar • 1 tbsp amaretto
For the cherry decoration: 100g (3½oz) cherry jam • 100g (3½oz) cherry purée (with 10% sugar, see p219) • 20g (¾oz) icing sugar • 1 tbsp cherry juice • 300g (10oz) fresh cherries, pitted
Equipment: piping bag with medium round nozzle

1. Preheat the oven to 160°C (325°F). Line 2 baking trays with baking parchment. To make the sponge, whisk the egg whites with the salt in a bowl using an electric hand whisk until they are stiff, gradually beating in the caster sugar as you do so. Sift the icing sugar and mix with the ground almonds and flour. Carefully fold this into the egg whites.

2. Spoon the batter into a piping bag fitted with a medium round nozzle and pipe 18 × 12cm (4½in) circles onto the tray, leaving a slight gap between each and starting in the centres, piping the mixture in an outward spiral until it is the desired size. Bake immediately on the middle shelf of the preheated oven for 20 minutes. Remove from the oven and leave to cool on the tray. Increase the oven temperature to 190°C (375°F/Gas 5).

3. For the crumble, mix the butter in a bowl with the flour, cocoa powder, light brown sugar, and vanilla seeds and rub with your fingertips to a rough crumble. Spread it over a baking tray lined with baking parchment and bake for around 10 minutes. Dust with icing sugar once it has cooled down.

4. To make the mascarpone cream, soak the gelatine in cold water for 10 minutes. Whip the cream in a bowl using an electric hand mixer until it is just holding its shape. Stir the mascarpone together with

the sugar in a bowl until it is creamy. Gently heat the amaretto in a pan, squeeze out the gelatine and dissolve it in the warmed amaretto. Stir about 2 tbsp of the mascarpone mixture into the amaretto, then swiftly stir this into the remaining mascarpone cream. Finally, carefully fold in the cream. Cover and refrigerate to set for 1 hour.

5. For each tartlet, spread 3 sponge bases with some cherry jam and mascarpone cream and layer them up. Put the remaining mascarpone cream in the cleaned piping bag fitted with a medium round nozzle and pipe a few blobs of cream on top each of the tartlets.

6. For the cherry decoration, stir together the cherry purée, icing sugar, and cherry juice and briefly bring to the boil. Leave to cool a little before dipping in the cherries. Decorate the tartlets with the dipped cherries and baked crumble.

Tip: crumble with a crunch
When making the crumble, take care that the pieces aren't too small. If you leave them larger they will have the right crunch once cooked.

▼

TIRAMISU

with amaretto mascarpone cream

For the tiramisu: **3 leaves of gelatine** • **750g (1lb 10oz) mascarpone** • **135g (4¾oz) caster sugar**
• **3 tbsp amaretto** • **450g (1lb) double cream** • **about 200g (7oz) sponge fingers, depending on the size of your container**
• **cocoa powder, for dusting**
For the coffee mixture: **500ml (18fl oz) lukewarm coffee or espresso** • **3 tbsp amaretto** • **60g (2oz) caster sugar**
Equipment: **30 × 20cm (12 × 8in) deep serving dish**

Serves 6   Prep: 20 mins + 4 hrs chilling

1. For the mascarpone cream, soak the gelatine for 10 minutes in cold water. Meanwhile, whisk the mascarpone and sugar together in a bowl using a balloon whisk until it has a smooth consistency.

2. Heat the amaretto in a pan, squeeze out the gelatine and dissolve it in the warmed amaretto. Stir in one-third of the mascarpone cream. Add this mixture to the remaining mascarpone cream in the bowl and whisk with the balloon whisk until everything is smooth.

3. Whip the cream in a bowl with an electric hand whisk on a medium setting until it is just holding its shape. Gradually fold into the mascarpone cream using the balloon whisk.

4. To make the coffee mixture, stir together the coffee, amaretto, and sugar. Dip the sponge fingers one at a time into the coffee mixture, soak them completely, then lay them close together in the serving dish until the base is covered.

5. Spread half the mascarpone cream evenly over the sponge finger base. Dip more of the sponge fingers into the coffee mixture and cover the mascarpone cream with them, pressing the sponge fingers down gently into the cream. Cover with the remaining mascarpone cream.

6. Cover the tiramisu with cling film and refrigerate for at least 4 hours and ideally 2 days. Dust with cocoa powder to serve.

Tip: keeping the coffee concoction
To make sure that the sponge fingers are properly soaked through with the coffee mixture, they must be completely dunked in the liquid. If you end up with some coffee mixture left over, refrigerate for 1–2 weeks in a sealed container.

▼

PROFITEROLES

with crunchy nougat

For the crunchy nougat: **flavourless vegetable oil, for the tray** • **15g (½oz) ground almonds** • **200g (7oz) caster sugar**
• **165g (5¾oz) almond nougat**
For the choux pastry: **4 tbsp milk** • **pinch of salt** • **1 tsp caster sugar** • **60g (2oz) unsalted butter**
• **75g (2½oz) plain flour** • **2 eggs** • **icing sugar, for dusting**
For the mascarpone cream: **1½ leaves of gelatine** • **125g (4½oz) double cream** • **250g (9oz) mascarpone**
• **1 tsp caster sugar** • **25g (scant 1oz) almond syrup (such as from Monin)**
Equipment: **piping bag with medium round nozzle**

Makes about 20   Prep: 1 hr + 1 hr chilling + cooling   Baking time: 20–30 mins

1. Prepare the crunchy nougat as described on p51. Preheat the oven to 180°C (350°F/Gas 4) and line a baking tray with baking parchment.

2. To make the choux pastry, bring the milk to the boil in a saucepan with 4 tbsp of water, the salt, sugar, and butter. Remove the saucepan from the hob, add the flour all at once and stir it in. Return the saucepan to the heat and dry out the dough for around 1 minute: stir over the heat until it clumps into a ball and a white residue has formed on the base of the saucepan.

3. Transfer the dough to a bowl. Whisk the eggs with a fork and gradually add to the still-warm dough mixture, beating constantly with an electric hand whisk on a low setting until a smooth, shiny consistency is achieved.

4. Spoon the dough into a piping bag fitted with a round nozzle and pipe 2–3cm (¾–1¼in) circles onto the baking parchment. Bake the profiteroles on the middle shelf of the hot oven for 20–30 minutes until golden brown. Leave to cool on a wire rack.

5. To make the mascarpone cream, soak the gelatine in cold water for 10 minutes. Meanwhile, whip the cream in a bowl using an electric hand whisk on a medium setting until it is just holding its shape. Stir the mascarpone with the sugar in a bowl. Gently heat the almond syrup in a saucepan, squeeze out the gelatine and dissolve it in the syrup. Stir 2 tbsp of the mascarpone mixture into the almond syrup mixture in the saucepan. Then quickly use a balloon whisk to combine this with the remaining mascarpone mixture. Take care that you don't get any lumps of gelatine. Finally, carefully fold in the cream. Cover and refrigerate to set for 1 hour.

6. To serve, split the profiteroles in half horizontally. Cut the crunchy nougat into little pieces and place a piece on each of the lower profiterole halves. Stir the mascarpone cream with the balloon whisk until smooth, transfer to the cleaned piping bag fitted with a medium round nozzle and pipe onto the lower profiterole sections. Replace the upper half of each profiterole and lightly dust with icing sugar.

▼

VIENNESE APPLE STRUDEL

with home-made strudel pastry

For the strudel pastry: 250g (9oz) plain flour, plus extra for dusting • 2 tbsp flavourless vegetable oil,
plus extra for coating the dough • icing sugar, for dusting
For the filling: 1kg (2lb 4oz) tart apples • 75g (2½oz) light brown sugar • 25g (scant 1oz) raisins
• 30g (1oz) almonds, chopped • seeds from 1 vanilla pod • finely grated zest and juice of ½ unwaxed lemon
• 130g (4¾oz) unsalted butter

Serves 6   Prep: 45 mins + 1 hr resting + cooling   Baking time: 30 mins

1. To make the strudel pastry, knead the flour with 150ml (5fl oz) cold water and the oil. You can do this in the bowl of a mixer fitted with a dough hook, or by hand, until you have a smooth, elastic dough. Shape the dough into a ball, coat with oil, wrap in cling film, and leave to rest for around 1 hour at room temperature.

2. In the meantime, work on the filling by peeling, quartering and coring the apples. Cut the apple quarters into thin slices and mix them in a bowl with the sugar, raisins, almonds, vanilla seeds, and lemon zest and juice. Melt the butter in a saucepan over a low heat.

3. Preheat the oven to 220°C (425°F/Gas 7) and line a baking tray with baking parchment. Roll out the pastry as thinly as possible on a large clean tea towel or linen strudel cloth (see tip) with just a little flour. Then stretch the pastry, working from the centre outwards until it is so wafer-thin that you could read a newspaper through it. To do this, put both hands under the pastry and stretch it little by little by pulling it outwards from the centre over the backs of your hands.

4. Spread the pastry with half the melted butter. Spread the apple filling lengthways over no more than one-third of the pastry sheet, leaving the edges free. Gently lift the towel on the side where the pastry is filled and gradually roll up the strudel using the cloth to help you. Press down the ends to seal.

5. With the help of the cloth, carefully lay the strudel seam-side down on the prepared baking tray. Bake for around 30 minutes on the middle shelf of the oven, brushing with the remaining melted butter after 15 minutes. Remove from the oven and serve lukewarm or cold, dusted with icing sugar.

Tip: the right cloth for strudel
In order to be able to roll up the wafer-thin strudel dough with the apple filling you will need the largest possible smooth tea towel (made from linen). You can buy special strudel cloths which are the perfect dimensions for strudel at around 120cm (48in) long. The dough is brushed with oil before it is rested, so it remains nicely elastic.

Tip: food processor for rye doughs
Doughs made with rye flour are heavier and stickier than wheat flour doughs. For this reason, kneading them by hand isn't recommended and – depending on how powerful it is – even a hand-held electric mixer may not be up to it. The best equipment for kneading these doughs is a food processor.

▼

FRUITED RYE LOAF

a traditional German recipe

For the marinated dried fruit: 250g (9oz) raisins • 70g (2¼oz) dried figs • 70g (2¼oz) dried apple • 40g (1¼oz) dried apricots • 2 tbsp rum
For the dough and sugar syrup: 20g (¾oz) fresh yeast • 400g (14oz) white rye flour, plus extra if needed • 1 tsp salt • 70g (2¼oz) hazelnuts • 50g (1¾oz) walnuts • 20g (¾oz) pine nuts • 20g (¾oz) candied orange peel, chopped • 20g (¾oz) candied lemon peel, chopped • ½ tsp mixed spice • 75g (2½oz) caster sugar

Makes 2   Prep: 25 mins + 24 hrs marinating + 1 hr resting + cooling   Baking time: 65–70 mins

1. The day before you make the bread, finely chop the raisins, figs, apples, and apricots and mix them with the rum in a bowl. Cover with cling film and weigh them down, for example with a cup. Leave to steep for 24 hours in the refrigerator.

2. The next day, dissolve the crumbled yeast in around 2 tbsp of lukewarm water. In a large bowl mix together the rye flour, salt, hazelnuts, walnuts, pine nuts, candied orange and lemon peel, mixed spice, yeasty water, and around 200ml (7fl oz) of warm water. Add the marinated dried fruit with its rum and knead everything together in a food processor fitted with a dough hook to form a dough (see tip). If necessary, add more water or flour to get a well formed dough that doesn't stick to your hands.

3. Divide in half and shape each into a round loaf. Cover with clean tea towels and leave to prove for 1 hour until they have clearly increased in size.

4. Preheat the oven to 160°C (325°F/Gas 3) and line 2 baking trays with baking parchment. Make a sugar syrup by bringing the sugar to the boil in a saucepan with 75ml (2½fl oz) of water. Put the fruit loaves onto the baking trays and bake them on the middle shelf of the oven for 65–70 minutes, brushing them with sugar syrup after 30 minutes and again after 45 minutes. Take the loaves out of the oven and leave to cool on a wire rack.

Tip: savoury variations
You can also dish these up as a savoury option. Slice the bread, melt a bit of butter in a frying pan, and toss the slices in sugar. Caramelize the slices in the brown butter and top each with goat's cheese. This is lovely with a glass of red wine.

Tip: storing the dough in the fridge
You can make the dough a
good couple of days before
baking, wrap in cling film, and
refrigerate until ready for use.

▼

LINZ BISCUITS

with raspberry jam

50g (1¾oz) salted butter, at room temperature • 140g (5oz) unsalted butter, at room temperature
• 130g (4½oz) caster sugar • 2 egg yolks • 200g (7oz) ground hazelnuts • 120g (4¼oz) plain flour
• seeds from 1 vanilla pod • pinch of ground cinnamon • small pinch of ground cloves • small pinch of salt
• about 250g (9oz) raspberry jam

Makes about 40   Prep: 20 mins + cooling   Baking time: 20 mins

1. Preheat the oven to 180°C (350°F/Gas 4) and line a baking tray with baking parchment.

2. Mix together both types of butter in a bowl with the sugar and egg yolks, using your hands or a mixer fitted with a dough hook. Add the hazelnuts, flour, vanilla seeds, cinnamon, cloves, and salt and knead everything swiftly together to a smooth consistency.

3. Make around 40 balls from the mix, each measuring 2–3cm (¾–1¼in) in diameter, and lay these on the baking tray. In the centre of each ball make a small impression, using your thumb or a wooden spoon handle. Fill each of these hollows generously with the raspberry jam to just below the upper rim (the jam contracts slightly when baked).

4. Bake the Linz biscuits on the middle shelf of the preheated oven for around 20 minutes until golden brown. Remove from the oven and leave to cool on a wire rack.

▼

SACHERTORTE

The Austrian classic

For the apricot jam (or just use apricot jam from a jar):
190g (6¾oz) apricots • 140g (5oz) granulated sugar • about 1 tbsp lemon juice
For the sponge and marzipan: 50g (1¾oz) unsalted butter • 50g (1¾oz) dark chocolate (ideally 67% cocoa solids)
• 6 eggs • 50g 1¾oz) plain flour • 25g (scant 1oz) cocoa powder • 215g (7½oz) good-quality marzipan
• 65g (2¼oz) icing sugar • 65g (2¼oz) caster sugar • 1 sheet of ready-rolled marzipan (see tip)
For the chocolate icing and decoration: 170g (5¾oz) dark chocolate (ideally couverture, see p218, for a shinier finish)
• 235g (8½oz) double cream • 200g (7oz) caster sugar • 85g (3oz) cocoa powder • 50g (1¾oz) white chocolate
Equipment: 26cm (10½in) cake ring or springform tin

Serves 8   Prep: 40 mins + 24 hrs marinating + cooling   Baking time: 6–7 mins

1. One day in advance, halve and pit the apricots for the jam. Chop into small cubes and toss with the sugar in a bowl, adding lemon juice to taste. Cover and leave to steep for 1 day. The following day, bring the mixture to the boil in a saucepan and simmer for at least 10 minutes over a low heat until it thickens. Leave to cool, cover, and refrigerate.

2. Preheat the oven to 180°C (350°F/Gas 4) and line a baking tray with baking parchment. To make the sponge, melt the butter and chocolate in a heatproof bowl over simmering water (don't let the bowl touch the water). Separate the eggs. Mix the flour and cocoa.

3. Chop the marzipan and mix with the icing sugar in a bowl using an electric hand whisk, gradually adding the egg yolks, 4 tbsp of water, and 2 of the egg whites, until a smooth consistency is achieved. Beat the remaining egg whites in a bowl with an electric hand whisk on a medium setting until stiff, gradually adding the caster sugar. Alternately fold the whisked egg whites, flour mixture, and melted chocolate into the marzipan mixture.

4. Spread the mixture over the baking tray so that it is about 1.5cm (½in) thick and bake on the middle shelf of the preheated oven for 6–7 minutes. Take care that the sponge doesn't dry out too much. Remove from the oven and leave to cool on the tray.

5. In the meantime, finely chop the chocolate for the icing and put it in a heatproof bowl. Bring 150g (5½oz) of the cream to the boil and pour it over the chocolate. Boil 250ml (9fl oz) of water in a saucepan with the sugar, add the cocoa and allow it to return to the boil. Add the remaining cream and let it come to the boil once more. Stir the cocoa mixture into the chocolate mix, incorporating as little air as possible. Cover, leave to cool down, then store in the refrigerator until ready for use.

6. To assemble the cake, use a cake ring or springform tin to stamp out 2 circles from the sponge. Lay one of the sponge bases in the cake ring or springform and spread it with half the apricot jam (save the rest for another occasion, or use on toast). Cover with the second sponge circle.

7. Remove the cake ring and cover the cake with the ready-rolled marzipan, pressing this down gently. Trim off any excess. Warm the chocolate icing very gently in a heatproof bowl over simmering water; it must on no account get too hot! Place the cake on a wire rack and cover with the icing. Melt the white chocolate as before, draw lines with it across the still-warm icing and use a toothpick to draw at right angles across the lines. Leave to cool before serving.

Tip: making marzipan covering
Larger supermarkets sell ready-rolled marzipan for covering cakes. If you can't get hold of this kind of marzipan covering, you can make your own quite easily instead. To do this, chop 250g (9oz) of good-quality marzipan into cubes, knead together with around 125g (4½oz) icing sugar and 1 tbsp rum and roll it out between sheets of baking parchment or cling film to form a disc around 5mm (¼in) thick.

Tip: good for preparing in advance
The shortcrust pastry lends itself
well to being prepared a day in
advance. Refrigerate until you
are ready to use it. The next day
prepare the topping and finish
making the nut wedges.

▼

NUT WEDGES

with a four nut combination

For the pastry: 275g (9½oz) icing sugar • 5 egg yolks • 450g (1lb) unsalted butter, chopped, plus extra for the tray • 670g (1½lb) plain flour • pinch of salt • 1 tsp vanilla powder • ½ tsp finely grated unwaxed lemon zest
For the nut topping and decoration: 100g (3½oz) pecans • 100g 3½oz) hazelnuts • 100g (3½oz) peanuts • 100g 3½oz) almonds • 170g (6oz) milk chocolate • 60g (2oz) dark chocolate (66% cocoa solids), plus 100g (3½oz) extra, for coating • 120g (4¼oz) unsalted butter • 125g (4½oz) caster sugar • 250g (9oz) liquid glucose (see p219) • 125g (4½oz) maple syrup • 2 tsp vanilla powder • 7 eggs • pinch of salt • 50g (1¾oz) white chocolate
Equipment: 40 × 30cm (16 × 12in) baking tray • baking beans, dried pulses, or raw rice

Makes 20   Prep: 50 mins + 2 hrs chilling + cooling   Baking time: 60–65 mins

1. To make the shortcrust pastry, swiftly knead together the icing sugar, egg yolks, butter, flour, salt, vanilla sugar, and lemon zest in a bowl, either by hand or using a mixer fitted with a dough hook, until you have a smooth dough. Shape into a ball, wrap in cling film and refrigerate for at least 2 hours.

2. Preheat the oven to 180°C (350°F/Gas 4). Butter the baking tray, roll out the shortcrust pastry to an even thickness on the tray and prick it all over with a fork. Line the pastry sheet with baking parchment and fill with baking beans for baking blind. Cook on the middle shelf for 10–15 minutes. Remove from the oven and take out the baking beans with the baking parchment. Reduce the oven temperature to 160°C (325°F/Gas 4).

3. To make the nut topping, coarsely chop the pecans, hazelnuts, peanuts, and almonds. Chop the milk and dark chocolate into little pieces, keeping them separate. Heat the butter in a saucepan with the sugar for around 1 minute, until the sugar has dissolved. Add half the milk chocolate and all the dark chocolate and stir everything together well.

4. Stir the liquid glucose in a separate saucepan with the maple syrup and vanilla powder until smooth. Stir the syrup into the chocolate mixture in a bowl. Add the eggs with the salt and mix using a hand-held blender. Finally, stir in the nuts and remaining chopped milk chocolate.

5. Spread the nutty mixture evenly over the shortcrust pastry base. Bake the whole thing on the middle shelf of the oven for around 50 minutes. Remove from the oven and leave to cool on the tray. Then cut into 10 × 6cm (4 × 2½in) pieces.

6. Melt the 100g (3½oz) dark chocolate and the white chocolate separately in heatproof bowls over simmering water (don't let the bowls touch the water). Dip the nut wedges into the dark chocolate on 2 sides. Decorate with lines of white chocolate.

Tip: chopping nuts
To chop the nuts, put them a few at a time on a large chopping board and use a large, sharp kitchen knife.

▼

SWISS NUT TARTLETS

with cranberries and white chocolate

Makes 6   Prep: 40 mins + 26 hrs chilling + cooling   Baking time: 20–25 mins

For the buttercream and decoration: 2 egg yolks • ½ sachet of vanilla blancmange mix • 100ml (3½fl oz) milk • 100g (3½oz) double cream • seeds from 1 vanilla pod • 15g (½oz) caster sugar • grated zest of ¼ unwaxed lemon • 6 tbsp cranberry jam • 100ml (3½fl oz) kirsch • 250g (9oz) unsalted butter • maraschino liqueur (optional) • 50g (1¾oz) white chocolate, for decoration • 50g (1¾oz) fresh cranberries, for decoration
For the pastry: 135g (4¾oz) unsalted butter, chopped, plus extra for the tins • 85g (3oz) icing sugar • 1 egg • 1 tsp vanilla powder • pinch of salt • seeds from ¼ vanilla pod • 30g (1oz) ground almonds • 225g (8oz) plain flour, plus extra for the tins
For the nut mixture: 40g (1¼oz) dark chocolate (66% cocoa solids) • 230g (8oz) white chocolate • 80g (2¾oz) unsalted butter • 85g (3oz) caster sugar • 165g (5¾oz) liquid glucose (see p219) • 125g (4½oz) maple syrup • 2 tsp vanilla powder • pinch of salt • 7 eggs • 130g (4¾oz) hazelnuts • 130g (4¾oz) almonds
Equipment: 6 × 10cm (4in) tartlet tins

1. One day in advance, start preparing the buttercream by mixing together the egg yolks and blancmange mix in a bowl with a balloon whisk. Put the milk in a pan with the cream, vanilla seeds, and sugar and bring to the boil, stirring constantly. Gradually pour the simmering milk mixture over the egg yolk mixture, stirring all the time. Put the whole thing back in the pan, bring briefly back to the boil again, stirring constantly, and allow to thicken. Press the mixture through a sieve and stir in the lemon zest. Cover with cling film, leave to cool, and refrigerate.

2. To make the shortcrust pastry, knead together the butter, sugar, egg, vanilla powder, salt, and vanilla seeds in the bowl of a mixer fitted with a dough hook. Add the ground almonds and flour and work everything swiftly together to form a smooth dough. Shape into a ball, press flat, wrap in cling film and refrigerate for at least 2 hours.

3. Lightly butter the tartlet tins and dust with flour, knocking out any excess.

4. Roll out the shortcrust pastry between 2 pieces of cling film to form a 5mm (¼in) thick round sheet and cut out 14cm (5½in) circles to line the tartlet tins. Trim any overhanging excess pastry edges and prick the pastry all over with a fork. Return to the refrigerator to chill for a further 30 minutes.

5. Preheat the oven to 190°C (375°F/Gas 5). To make the nut mixture, finely chop the dark and white chocolate separately. Melt the butter with the sugar in a saucepan and cook for 1 minute. Remove from the heat and stir in the dark chocolate along with half the white chocolate until they have melted.

6. Put the liquid glucose in a saucepan with the maple syrup and vanilla powder and boil until they form a syrup. Stir the syrup into the butter and chocolate mixture in a bowl. Add the salt and gradually mix in the eggs with an electric hand whisk. Chop the hazelnuts and almonds and mix these in with the remaining white chocolate.

7. Spread the shortcrust pastry bases with cranberry jam, cover with the nut mixture and smooth this out. Bake on the lowest shelf in the oven for 20–25 minutes, then remove and drizzle with the kirsch.

8. To make the buttercream, beat the butter until it is pale. Gradually beat in the well-chilled vanilla blancmange. Finally, add the maraschino liqueur to taste and spread over the tartlets. When you are ready to serve, coarsely grate the white chocolate. Garnish the tartlets with the grated chocolate and jewel-like cranberries.

Tip: store in the freezer
The finished whole tart freezes
beautifully. Put the tart on a
firm base and slide the whole
thing into a freezer bag. To
defrost, remove from the bag
and place in the refrigerator.

▼

SWEDISH ALMOND CAKE

with a German twist

For the almond layers: **5 egg whites** • **120g (4¼oz) caster sugar** • **150g (5½oz) ground almonds**
For the cream: **4 leaves of gelatine** • **5 egg yolks** • **100g (3½oz) double cream** • **60g (2oz) caster sugar**
• **175g (6oz) unsalted butter**
For the icing: **400g (14oz) white chocolate** • **100ml (3½fl oz) flavourless vegetable oil**
For the caramelized almonds: **25g (scant 1oz) each whole and chopped almonds** • **50g (1¾oz) icing sugar**

Serves 12   Prep: 30 mins + 1 hr chilling + cooling   Baking time: 20 mins

1. Preheat the oven to 180°C (350°F/Gas 4) with the fan on. Draw 2 × 25cm (10in) circles on baking parchment and lay each on a separate baking tray.

2. To make the almond layers, whisk the egg whites in a bowl using an electric hand whisk until they are stiff. Carefully fold in the sugar and ground almonds.

3. Divide the almond mixture equally between the baking paper circles and smooth it out. Bake on the middle shelf of the preheated oven for 20 minutes. Halfway through the baking time, switch the trays around so that both cook evenly. Remove from the oven, turn out onto a chopping board and carefully remove the baking parchment. Leave to cool.

4. Meanwhile, soak the gelatine for the cream in cold water for 10 minutes. Stir together the egg yolks, cream, and sugar in a pan. Bring the mixture to the boil, then stir constantly over a medium-low heat to simmer and thicken. Squeeze out the gelatine and dissolve it in this mixture. Remove from the heat and leave to cool slightly. Chop the butter and gradually stir it in. Cover the surface with cling film and refrigerate for around 1 hour.

5. Spread half the cream over an almond disc, lay the other on top and cover completely with the remaining cream.

6. To make the icing, coarsely chop the chocolate and melt it with the oil in a heatproof bowl over simmering water (don't let the bowl touch the water), stirring to combine. Use to cover the cake.

7. For the caramelized nuts, preheat the oven to 190°C (375°F/Gas 5). Toast the almonds on a baking tray in the centre of the preheated oven for around 8 minutes. Add them to a saucepan, sprinkle with the icing sugar, and let them caramelize, stirring constantly. Decorate the cake with the almonds.

▼

DUTCH CREAM CAKE

with strawberries and cream

For the puff pastry (basic pastry or détrempe): 40g (1¼oz) unsalted butter • 1 tsp salt • 250g (9oz) plain flour
For the puff pastry (beurrage): 160g (5¾oz) unsalted butter • 50g (1¾oz) plain flour • 1 egg yolk
For the shortcrust pastry: 90g (3oz) unsalted butter, chopped • 55g (1¾oz) icing sugar • 1 egg • pinch of salt
• seeds from ½ vanilla pod • 150g (5½oz) plain flour • 20g (¾oz) ground almonds
For the cherry filling: 720ml jar of pitted Morello cherries • 30g (1oz) cornflour • 75g (2½oz) caster sugar
• 1 tsp vanilla powder • 1 cinnamon stick • 2 large strips of unwaxed lemon zest
For the cream filling: 500g (1lb 2oz) double cream • 50g (1¾oz) caster sugar • 1 tsp vanilla powder
• seeds from 2 vanilla pods • 3 sheets of gelatin• 3 tbsp rum
To assemble: 50g (1¾oz) dark chocolate • 2–3 tbsp cherry jam • 150g (5½oz) strawberries, sliced
• 2–3 tbsp strawberry jam • about 50g (1¾oz) bought glacé icing or poured fondant icing (see p219)
Equipment: 26cm (10½in) cake ring • piping bag with round nozzle

Serves 12–16   Prep: 1 hr + 30 hrs chilling + cooling   Baking time: 35–40 mins

1. One day in advance, prepare the mix for the puff pastry base (détrempe) as described (see p216).

2. The following day prepare the beurrage as described (see p216) and chill.

3. In the meantime, work on the shortcrust pastry, kneading together the butter, icing sugar, egg, salt, and vanilla seeds in a bowl of a mixer fitted with a dough hook. Add the flour and ground almonds and work everything swiftly to a smooth consistency. Shape the pastry into a ball, press flat, wrap in cling film and refrigerate for around 2 hours.

4. To finish making the puff pastry, work the détrempe and the beurrage as described (see p216), rolling out, folding together (single and double folds), and chilling as described.

5. During the final chilling period, drain the Morello cherries over a bowl, reserving their juice. Stir the cornflour with 3–4 tbsp of the cherry juice until smooth. Put the remaining cherry juice into a saucepan with the sugar, vanilla powder, cinnamon stick, and lemon zest and bring to the boil. Remove the cinnamon and lemon zest. Add the cornflour mixture to thicken the cherry juice mixture, stirring well. Fold in the cherries and leave to cool.

6. Preheat the oven to 190°C (375°F/Gas 5) and line a baking tray with baking parchment. Roll out the shortcrust pastry to around 5mm (¼in) thick and use the cake ring to stamp out a 26cm (10½in) circle. Lay the pastry disc on the baking tray, prick it all over with a fork and bake on the middle shelf of the preheated oven for around 8 minutes until golden brown. Remove and leave to cool on a wire rack.

7. Increase the oven temperature to 220°C (425°F/Gas 7). Roll out the puff pastry to around 7mm (⅓in) thick and stamp out a 26cm (10½in) circle. Lay the pastry circle flipped over on the baking tray and brush the surface with egg yolk. No egg yolk should get on the stamped-out edge of the pastry as this

would impede its rise during baking. Bake the puff pastry sheet on the middle shelf of the preheated oven for around 30 minutes until golden brown, baking any leftover puff pastry remnants alongside. Remove from the oven and leave to cool on a wire rack. Split the puff pastry sheet in half horizontally to get 2 layers.

8. To make the cream filling, whip the cream with the sugar, vanilla powder, and vanilla seeds in a bowl using an electric hand whisk on a medium setting until it is just holding its shape. Soak the gelatin in cold water, squeeze it. Heat the rum a little, then dissolve the gelatin in the rum. Fold the rum into the whipped cream.

9. Melt the couverture chocolate in a heatproof bowl over simmering water (don't let the bowl touch the water). Place the cake ring on a baking sheet around the shortcrust base. Brush the base with a thick layer of chocolate, then the cherry jam, cover with strawberries, spread with some of the cream filling, lay a puff pastry sheet on top and spread with the cherry filling. Reserve some of the cream filling in the refrigerator for decoration and spread the remainder smoothly over the cherry filling. Chill the cake for at least 4 hours in the refrigerator.

10. Heat the strawberry jam in a small saucepan and brush it over the second puff pastry sheet. Warm the glacé icing or fondant in the same way and spread it over the jam. Use a spoon to draw some swirls, thus creating the marbled effect. Decorate the sides of the cake with the crumbled puff pastry remnants. Cut the iced puff pastry sheet into 12–16 portions, depending on the desired size.

11. Release the cake from the ring mould. Fill a piping bag fitted with a round nozzle with the reserved cream filling and pipe blobs of cream onto the edges of the cake. Lay the iced puff pastry pieces at an angle on the blobs of cream.

▼
SPECIAL
&
UNUSUAL

Introducing the exotic flavours of
green tea, sesame, lychee, lemon verbena,
or yuzu… if you really want to
wake up your taste buds, you
can't go wrong with the recipes
in this chapter.

▼

EXOTIC MUFFINS

with mango and passion fruit

For the muffins: 100g (3½oz) unsalted butter, at room temperature, plus extra for the moulds (optional) • 80g (2¾oz) caster sugar • seeds from ½ vanilla pod • pinch of salt • 2 eggs • 100g (3½oz) banana • 100g (3½oz) mango • 65g (5¾oz) passion fruit purée (with 10% sugar, see p219), or passion fruit nectar, or passion fruit smoothie • 4 tbsp lime juice • 310g (10¼oz) plain flour • 2½ tsp baking powder • icing sugar, for dusting (optional)
Equipment: 12-hole muffin tray • 12 paper muffin cases (optional)

Makes 12   Prep: 30 mins + cooling   Baking time: 30 mins

1. Preheat the oven to 180°C (350°F/Gas 4). Butter the muffin moulds, or insert a paper case into each.

2. To make the muffins, cream the butter with half the sugar, the vanilla seeds, and salt in a bowl using an electric hand whisk. Separate the eggs. Gradually add the egg yolks one at a time to the butter and sugar mixture, beating just enough after each addition to combine the ingredients.

3. Roughly chop the banana and mango into pieces and put them with the passion fruit purée and lime juice in a high-sided beaker. Purée well with a hand-held blender. Stir the fruit purée into the butter and sugar mixture. Combine the flour and baking powder and sift this into the mixture, stirring just enough to produce a smooth

consistency. Whisk the egg whites until they are stiff, gradually adding the remaining sugar as you do so. Fold the whisked egg whites gradually into the muffin mix.

4. Divide the batter evenly between the moulds or cases. Bake on the middle shelf of the preheated oven for around 30 minutes until golden brown. Remove from the oven and leave to cool in the tin. To serve, dust with icing sugar (if using).

Tip: fully ripe fruit
It is crucial to use completely ripe bananas and mangoes for this recipe, as only then will the fruits impart their fragrant exotic flavours.

▼

RED BERRY COMPOTE CUPCAKES

Pâtisserie style

Makes 12   Prep: 40 mins + 24 hrs chilling + cooling   Baking time: 20–25 mins

For the ganache: 125g (4½oz) white chocolate • 200g (7oz) double cream • 1 tsp liquid glucose

For the compote: 25g (scant 1oz) raspberries, fresh or thawed from frozen • 25g (scant 1oz) pitted sour cherries, fresh or thawed from frozen • 25g (scant 1oz) redcurrants, fresh or thawed from frozen • 25g (scant 1oz) blackberries, fresh or thawed from frozen • 25g (scant 1oz) blueberries, fresh or thawed from frozen • 125ml (4fl oz) raspberry juice • 1 tbsp vanilla blancmange mix • 2 tbsp caster sugar

For the cake and decoration: unsalted butter, for the moulds (optional) • 165g (5¾oz) caster sugar • 3 large eggs • seeds from 1 vanilla pod • 1 tsp vanilla powder • 185ml (6fl oz) flavourless vegetable oil • 165g (5¾oz) plain flour • 1 tsp baking powder • 80g (2¾oz) mixed berries, thawed from frozen • fresh berries, for decoration

For the chocolate sauce: 1 tbsp liquid glucose • 15g (½oz) cocoa powder • 10g (¼oz) dark chocolate, chopped

Equipment: piping bag with medium round nozzle • 12-hole muffin tray • 12 paper muffin cases (optional)

1. One day in advance, finely chop the chocolate for the white ganache and put it in a heatproof bowl. Bring 125g (4½oz) of the cream to the boil in a saucepan with the glucose, pour it over the chocolate and leave to stand for 2 minutes. Mix with a hand-held blender or spatula, gradually adding the remaining cream. Take care not to incorporate any air. Cover and refrigerate for at least 24 hours.

2. The following day, whip the ganache with an electric hand whisk on a medium setting until you have a dense, smooth cream. Spoon it into a piping bag fitted with a medium round nozzle and refrigerate until ready for use.

3. To make the red berry compote, put three-quarters of the fruit in a large saucepan with 80ml (2½fl oz) of the raspberry juice and bring to the boil. Mix the remaining raspberry juice with the blancmange powder and sugar. Add this mixture to the fruit and juice mixture, stirring constantly, and return briefly to the boil to thicken. Leave to cool down to room temperature, then carefully fold in the remaining fruit. Cover and refrigerate until ready for use.

4. Preheat the oven to 190°C (375°F/Gas 5). Butter the muffin moulds, or insert a paper case into each.

5. To make the cake, use a balloon whisk to smoothly combine the sugar, eggs, vanilla seeds, vanilla powder, and oil in a bowl. Mix the flour with the baking powder and stir this into the sugar mixture just enough to combine well. Fold in the mixed berries.

6. Divide the batter evenly between the moulds. Bake on the middle shelf of the preheated oven for 20–25 minutes until golden brown. Remove from the oven and leave to cool in the tin.

7. To make the chocolate sauce, bring the glucose to the boil in a saucepan with 75ml (2½fl oz) of water and stir in the cocoa powder and chocolate. Shortly before serving, pipe blobs of white ganache onto the cupcakes and decorate with fresh berries, compote and a drizzle of chocolate sauce.

▼

HONEYED CUPCAKES

with almond crunch

Makes 12   Prep: 40 mins + 1 hr chilling + cooling   Baking time: 20–30 mins

For the filling: 5 egg yolks • 1 sachet of vanilla blancmange mix • 250ml (9fl oz) milk • 400g (14oz) double cream • seeds from 1 vanilla pod • 75g (2½oz) caster sugar • ½ tsp finely grated unwaxed lemon zest • 1½ leaves of gelatine
For the cakes: unsalted butter, for the moulds (optional) • 165g (5¾oz) caster sugar • 3 large eggs • seeds from ½ vanilla pod • 185ml (6¼fl oz) flavourless vegetable oil • 165g (5¾oz) plain flour • 2 tsp baking powder
For the almond crunch and decoration: 55g (2oz) unsalted butter • 25g (scant 1oz) honey • 20g (¾oz) liquid glucose • 30g (1oz) caster sugar • 70g (2¼oz) double cream • 75g (2½oz) flaked almonds • icing sugar, for dusting
Equipment: 12-hole muffin tray • 12 paper muffin cases (optional) • piping bag with medium round nozzle

1. To make the vanilla cream filling, mix the egg yolks and blancmange in a bowl with a balloon whisk. Put the milk in a saucepan with 250g (9oz) of the cream, the vanilla seeds, and sugar, bring to the boil, then gradually pour into the egg yolk mixture, stirring constantly. Return the mixture to the saucepan and return briefly to the boil, stirring all the time, until it thickens. Strain through a fine sieve. Stir in the lemon zest, cover, and refrigerate.

2. Preheat the oven to 190°C (375°F/Gas 5). Butter the muffin moulds, or insert a paper case into each. To make the cake, use a balloon whisk to combine the sugar, eggs, vanilla seeds, and oil in a bowl. Mix together the flour and baking powder and stir this in too. Divide evenly between the moulds.

3. To make the almond crunch, simmer the butter with the honey, glucose, sugar, and cream in a saucepan for at least 2 minutes, then fold in the almonds. Spread one-third of the almond mixture onto the cakes. Bake on the middle shelf of the preheated oven for 20–30 minutes. Remove from the oven and leave to rest for another 5 minutes in the tin. Then transfer the cupcakes to a wire rack to cool. Don't turn off the oven.

4. Spread the remaining almond mixture over a baking tray lined with baking parchment and bake in the oven for around 10 minutes until golden brown. Let the mixture cool, then break into pieces.

5. Meanwhile, return to the filling. Soak the gelatine in cold water for 10 minutes. Whip the remaining 150g (5½oz) of cream in a bowl using an electric hand whisk on a medium setting until it is just holding its shape. Use a balloon whisk to stir the blancmange mixture until it is smooth again. Lift out the gelatine from its soaking water and dissolve it in a little saucepan over a low heat. Swiftly stir it into the blancmange. Gradually fold in the cream, cover, and refrigerate for 1 hour.

6. Shortly before serving, use the balloon whisk to stir the cream again until it is smooth and transfer it to a piping bag fitted with a round nozzle. Decorate the cupcakes with the vanilla cream. If desired, you can slice the cupcakes horizontally into 3 and pipe each piece with cream, before sandwiching together to create a layered effect, as in the photograph. Top with the almond crunch, and dust with icing sugar.

Tip: extra chocolatey
If you're the kind of person who can't get enough chocolate, dip the corners of the slices into chocolate once they have cooled down. To do this, melt 200g (7oz) dark chocolate, dip the corner of each slice into the melted chocolate, then leave to set on baking parchment.

▼

PECAN SLICES

with caramel chocolate

For the shortbread: 270g (9½oz) icing sugar • 5 egg yolks • 450g (1lb) unsalted butter, chopped, plus extra for the tray • 670g (1½lb) plain flour • ¼ tsp salt • 1 tsp vanilla powder • ½ tsp finely grated unwaxed lemon zest
For the topping and decoration: 400g (14oz) pecans • 170g (6oz) caramel-flavoured chocolate, or milk chocolate • 170g (6oz) milk chocolate • 60g (2oz) dark chocolate (66% cocoa solids) • 120g (4¼oz) unsalted butter • 140g (5oz) caster sugar • 250g (9oz) liquid glucose • 125g (4½oz) maple syrup • 1½ tsp vanilla powder • 7 eggs • pinch of salt • white chocolate, chopped, for decoration • pecans, chopped, for decoration • milk chocolate shavings, for decoration
Equipment: baking beans, dried pulses, or raw rice

Makes about 20   Prep: 50 mins + 2 hrs chilling + cooling   Baking time: 60–65 mins

1. To make the shortbread, knead the icing sugar, egg yolks, butter, flour, salt, vanilla powder, and lemon zest in a bowl, either by hand or using a mixer fitted with a dough hook, working swiftly until smooth. Shape into a ball, press flat, wrap in cling film, and refrigerate for around 2 hours.

2. Preheat the oven to 180°C (350°F/Gas 4). Butter a baking tray. Roll the dough out evenly on the baking tray and prick it all over with a fork. Line with baking parchment and weigh this down with baking beans. Bake on the middle shelf of the preheated oven for 10–15 minutes. Remove the baking beans and baking parchment. Reduce the oven temperature to 160°C (325°F/Gas 3).

3. To make the topping, roughly chop the pecans. Separately chop the caramel chocolate, milk chocolate, and dark chocolate finely. Boil the butter and sugar in a saucepan for 1 minute until the sugar dissolves. Stir in the milk and dark chocolate.

4. In a separate saucepan, stir together the glucose, maple syrup, and vanilla powder, and bring to the boil. Stir this into the chocolate mixture. Allow to cool slightly, then add the eggs with the salt and mix thoroughly using a hand-held blender. Finally, add the chopped nuts and caramel chocolate.

5. Spread the mixture evenly over the shortbread base. Cook on the middle shelf of the oven for around 50 minutes. Remove from the oven and leave to cool on the tray. Then cut into 10 × 6cm (4 × 2½in) pieces.

6. Preheat the oven to 190°C (375°F/Gas 5). Melt the white chocolate in the oven for 10 minutes, allow to cool, then dab dry with kitchen paper. Decorate the pecan slices with pecans, chocolate shavings, and caramelized white chocolate.

▼

YEASTED APPLE CAKE

with hazelnut streusel

For the yeast dough: **75ml (2½fl oz)** milk, plus extra if needed • **20g (¾oz)** fresh yeast • **40g (1¼oz)** caster sugar • **250g (9oz)** plain flour, plus extra if needed and for dusting • **90g (3oz)** unsalted butter, melted, plus extra for the tin • **1 tbsp** flavourless oil • pinch of salt • **1** egg • seeds from **½** vanilla pod • finely grated zest of **½** unwaxed lemon
For the crème pâtissière: **65g (2¼oz)** caster sugar • **2–3** egg yolks • **30g (1oz)** vanilla blancmange mix • **½** vanilla pod • **250ml (9fl oz)** milk
For the hazelnut streusel: **65g (2¼oz)** unsalted butter, at room temperature • **65g (2¼oz)** light brown sugar • pinch of salt • seeds from **½** vanilla pod • **130g (4¾oz)** ground hazelnuts • **30g (1oz)** chopped hazelnuts
For the apple purée and decoration: **3** apples, about **400g (14oz)** in total, plus **3** apples, peeled and sliced • **65g (2¼oz)** caster sugar • **2 tbsp** apple juice • **1 tbsp** caramel syrup (such as from Monin) • **½** vanilla pod • **½** cinnamon stick • Chantilly Cream (optional, see p62) • icing sugar, for dusting
Equipment: **28cm (11in)** springform tin

Serves 16   Prep: 1 hr + 1½ hrs resting + cooling   Baking time: 40 mins

1. To make the yeast dough, heat the milk until it is lukewarm. Crumble in the yeast and stir in the sugar until the yeast dissolves. Put the flour into a large bowl and make a well in the centre. Pour the yeasted milk into the well and mix to a paste with the flour. Cover with a clean tea towel and leave to prove for around 30 minutes at room temperature until it has nearly doubled in volume.

2. Stir in the melted butter with the oil, salt, egg, vanilla seeds, and lemon zest and knead everything to a smooth elastic dough which comes away from the sides of the bowl. If necessary, add a touch more milk or flour. Cover and once again leave the dough to prove for around 30 minutes until it has doubled in volume.

3. Meanwhile, prepare the various cake toppings. Make the crème pâtissière as described (see p158) and leave to cool.

4. For the streusel, use your hands, or a mixer fitted with a dough hook, to work the butter, sugar, salt, vanilla seeds, and both ground and chopped nuts to a crumble. Cover and refrigerate.

5. To make the apple purée, peel, halve and core the 3 apples and finely chop the fruit. Boil the sugar in a saucepan with 3 tbsp of water until you have a dark caramel. Add the apple pieces and immediately the apple juice and caramel syrup. Slice the vanilla pod lengthways and scrape out the seeds, adding both seeds and pod to the saucepan with the cinnamon. Simmer gently until the apples become a pulp. Remove the vanilla pod and cinnamon stick and purée the mixture well with a hand-held blender. Leave to cool down in a bowl.

6. Butter the springform tin. Knead the yeasted dough briefly once again and spread it out evenly in the tin. Stir the crème pâtissière with a balloon whisk and spread it over the dough base, then arrange the 3 sliced apples and then the apple purée on top. Finally, scatter over the streusel. Cover and leave to prove again for 20–30 minutes until the volume of the dough has increased by about one-third. Meanwhile, preheat the oven to 180°C (350°F/Gas 4).

7. Bake the cake on the middle shelf of the preheated oven for around 40 minutes until golden brown. Remove from the oven and let it cool completely in the tin. Decorate with blobs of Chantilly cream (if using), and dust with icing sugar.

Tip: can be prepared in advance
The crème pâtissière, hazelnut streusel, and apple purée can all be made 1–2 days ahead, covered, and refrigerated until ready for use. Then just prepare the dough, add the toppings, and bake.

▼

GREEN TEA BROWNIES

with macadamia nuts

600g (1lb 5oz) unsalted butter, plus extra for the tray • 125g (4½oz) plain flour • 60g (2oz) cocoa powder
• 60g (2oz) green tea powder (matcha, from a tea shop or Asian store), plus extra for dusting
• 400g (14oz) white chocolate • 11 eggs • 45g (1½oz) caster sugar • 400g (14oz) light brown sugar
• 3½ tbsp hazelnut oil, or flavourless vegetable oil • 200g (7oz) macadamia nuts • icing sugar, for dusting

Makes 20   Prep: 45 mins + cooling   Baking time: 40 mins

1. Preheat the oven to 200°C (400°F/Gas 6) and butter a baking tray. Sift the flour together with the cocoa powder and tea powder. Chop the butter and chocolate finely. Melt both together in a heatproof bowl suspended over simmering water (don't let the bowl touch the water).

2. Beat the eggs, caster sugar, and light brown sugar in a bowl using an electric hand whisk until creamy. Gradually stir in the warm butter and chocolate and the oil. Carefully fold in the flour mixture. Chop the nuts and fold them in.

3. Spread the mixture over the baking tray and smooth it out. Bake on the middle shelf of the preheated oven for around 40 minutes. Remove from the oven and leave to cool in the tray.

4. To serve, slice into 5cm (2in) square brownies and sift over some green tea powder and icing sugar. If you like, scatter some caramelized macadamia nuts over the brownies or drizzle with caramel sauce (see tip, right).

Tip: use as a base
The brownie in all its various forms is an excellent base for a spectacular fruit-topped large cake. Just bake the brownie as normal and then stamp out the required shape, or prepare it directly in a round tin. Then glaze with whatever variety of chocolate you like and top with a thick layer of fruit, such as apples, raspberries, or blueberries.

Tip, decorating options
The brownies can also be decorated with caramelized macadamia nuts. These are prepared exactly like the caramelized hazelnuts (see p191). The brownies also look stunning when decorated with caramel sauce (see p43).

▼

POPPY SEED TART

with pears

For the pastry: 150g (5½oz) unsalted butter, chopped, plus extra for the tin • 100g (3½oz) icing sugar
• 30g (1oz) ground almonds • 1 egg • 250g (9oz) plain flour, plus extra for dusting
For the topping and decoration: 90g (3oz) durum wheat semolina • 90g (3oz) ground poppy seeds,
plus extra for decoration • 40g (1¼oz) ground almonds • pinch of ground cinnamon • pinch of salt
• 670ml (1¼ pints) milk • 40g (1¼oz) unsalted butter • 120g (4¼oz) caster sugar • seeds from 1 vanilla pod
• 1 large egg • 4 ripe pears • Chantilly Cream (see p62) • flaked almonds, for decoration • 2 tbsp icing sugar
Equipment: 26cm (10½in) tart tin • baking beans, dried pulses, or raw rice

Serves 12   Prep: 30 mins + 2 hrs chilling + cooling   Baking time: 40–50 mins

1. To make the shortcrust pastry, mix the butter and icing sugar in the bowl of a mixer fitted with a dough hook. Knead in first the almonds and then the egg. Finally, sift in the flour and work all the ingredients swiftly together to a smooth consistency. Shape the pastry into a ball, press flat, wrap in cling film, and refrigerate for at least 2 hours.

2. Preheat the oven to 180°C (350°F/Gas 4) and butter the tin. Roll out the pastry on a lightly floured work surface or between 2 sheets of cling film until it is about 5mm (¼in) thick and then use it to line the tin. Trim any overhanging pastry edges and prick the pastry base all over with a fork.

3. Blind-bake the pastry on the middle shelf of the preheated oven for around 10 minutes, as described (see p59). Remove the baking beans with the baking parchment and continue baking the tart base for 10–12 minutes until golden brown. Remove the shortcrust pastry from the oven and leave to cool in the tin. Increase the oven temperature to 210°C (410°F/Gas 6½).

4. Meanwhile, prepare the topping by combining the semolina with the poppy seeds, almonds, cinnamon, and salt. Bring the milk to the boil in a pan with the butter, caster sugar, and vanilla seeds. Add the semolina mixture, stirring all the time, and bring to the boil. Remove from the heat and beat with an electric hand whisk to cool it down. When the mixture is only just warm, stir in the egg.

5. Peel the pears and slice each into 8, removing the cores. Lay out the pear slices in a fan shape on the pastry base and smooth the semolina mixture evenly over the top. Knock the tin gently several times on the work surface remove any air bubbles.

6. Bake the cake in the centre of the oven for around 20 minutes. Remove from the oven, leave to cool in the tin, and then remove it from the tin. Mix the Chantilly cream with the poppy seeds for decoration. Spread this around the edge of the cake and sprinkle with flaked almonds. Mix the icing sugar with 1 tsp water and drizzle this onto the almonds to serve.

▼

CRONUTS

with yuzu jelly and vanilla cream filling

Makes about 10
Prep: 70 mins + 3 hrs resting + 40 mins frying + chilling

For the puff pastry (yeasted dough) and for frying: 500g (1lb 2oz) plain flour, plus extra for dusting • ½ tsp salt • 200ml (7fl oz) milk • 70g (2¼oz) caster sugar • 30g (1oz) fresh yeast • 1 egg • 30g (1oz) unsalted butter, at room temperature • 2 litres (3½ pints) flavourless vegetable oil, for frying • 4 tbsp icing sugar

For the puff pastry (beurrage): 400g (14oz) unsalted butter • 120g (4¼oz) plain flour

For the vanilla cream: 60g (2oz) caster sugar • 3 egg yolks • 25g (scant 1oz) vanilla blancmange mix • ½ vanilla pod • 250ml (9fl oz) milk

For the yuzu jelly: 350ml (12fl oz) yuzu sake (from a mail order company, delicatessen, or Asian store) • 125ml (4fl oz) apple juice • 1 heaped tsp agar agar

Equipment: 8cm (3in) round doughnut cutter, or 4cm (1½in) and 8cm (3in) round cutters • kitchen thermometer (optional) • 2 piping bags with medium round nozzles

1. To make the cronuts, prepare the yeasted dough and the beurrage, (see p217), and leave to prove or chill, as appropriate.

2. Meanwhile, prepare the fillings. For the vanilla cream, stir one third of the sugar with the egg yolks and the vanilla blancmange mix in a bowl. Cut the vanilla pod lengthways and scrape out the seeds with a knife. Put the seeds and the pod in a saucepan with the milk and remaining sugar and bring to the boil, stirring constantly. Remove the vanilla pod and pour the hot milk into the egg yolk mixture, stirring all the time with a balloon whisk. Return the mixture to the pan and return to the boil briefly to thicken. Transfer immediately into a cold container, cover the surface with cling film and refrigerate.

3. To make the yuzu jelly, boil the sake, apple juice, and agar agar in a saucepan for around 2 minutes (check the package instructions for the precise cooking time). Leave to cool and refrigerate until set. Then cut into pieces, transfer to a high-sided beaker and purée until smooth with a hand-held blender. Cover the jelly and refrigerate.

4. Proceed with the yeasted dough and beurrage, as described (see p217): roll out, fold together (single and double folds), and chill as specified. Then roll out the dough to form a 3–4mm (¼in) thick sheet and stamp out 8cm (3in) rings with the cutter or cutters. Turn the rings over, cover, and let them rest in the refrigerator for 10 minutes.

5. Meanwhile, heat the oil for frying in a high-sided pan to 180°C (350°F), and keep the temperature stable. Use a kitchen thermometer, or hold a wooden spoon handle in the oil: the oil is hot enough when tiny bubbles rise up it. Cook the dough rings carefully, in batches, in the hot oil for 4 minutes on both sides until golden brown, turning with a slotted spoon. Remove with a slotted spoon, let them drain, and lay them on kitchen paper to blot off the oil.

6. To fill the cronuts, use a balloon whisk to vigorously stir the chilled vanilla cream until it is smooth and push it through a fine sieve. Likewise, stir the yuzu jelly until it is smooth. Put each filling into a piping bag fitted with a medium round nozzle. Cut the cronuts in half horizontally. Alternately pipe blobs of each of the 2 fillings onto the lower half of each cronut, then set the upper halves on top.

6. Mix the icing sugar with just enough water to form a glaze, then glaze the top of the cronuts.

▼

BLUEBERRY CAKE

with crème pâtissière

For the crème pâtissière: 80g (2¾oz) caster sugar • 3 egg yolks • 1 heaped tbsp vanilla blancmange powder
• ½ vanilla pod • 330ml (11fl oz) milk
For the cake: 300g (10oz) unsalted butter • 200g (7oz) buckwheat flour (see tip) • 2 tsp baking powder
• 500g (1lb 2oz) light brown sugar • 200g (7oz) ground almonds • pinch of salt • 500g (1lb 2oz) egg whites,
at room temperature (from a carton) • 500g (1lb 2oz) blueberries, fresh or thawed from frozen,
plus more fresh blueberries for decoration • icing sugar, for dusting
Equipment: 30 × 20cm (12 × 8in) deep rectangular baking tin, or 26cm (10½in) springform tin
• piping bag with medium round nozzle

Serves 12–15   Prep: 40 mins + cooling   Baking time: 45 mins

1. For the crème pâtissière, stir together 1 tbsp of the sugar with the egg yolks and blancmange mix in a bowl using a balloon whisk. Use a knife to slice the vanilla pod in half lengthways and scrape out the seeds. Bring the milk to the boil in a saucepan with the vanilla pod, seeds, and the remaining sugar, stirring constantly. Remove the vanilla pod and pour the boiling milk onto the egg yolk mixture, stirring vigorously. Return this mixture to the saucepan and stir constantly while returning briefly to the boil. Transfer immediately to a cold bowl, cover the surface with cling film, and leave to cool.

2. Preheat the oven to 180°C (350°F/Gas 4) and line the base of the baking tin with baking parchment. To make the cake, melt the butter in a saucepan over a medium heat until it is golden brown. Remove the saucepan from the hob and let the butter cool slightly; it will continue to brown a little.

3. Combine the buckwheat flour, baking powder, light brown sugar, almonds, and salt in a bowl. Add the egg whites and butter and beat everything until

smooth with an electric hand whisk. Transfer the mixture to the baking tin and smooth it out. Distribute the 500g (1lb 2oz) blueberries evenly over the mixture and press them in gently.

4. Bake the cake for 15 minutes on the middle shelf of the preheated oven. During this time, stir the crème pâtissière with a balloon whisk until smooth again, press it through a fine sieve and transfer to a piping bag fitted with a medium round nozzle.

5. Take the cake out of the oven and pipe in the crème pâtissière at regular intervals of around 2cm (¾in). Don't pipe in too much, it should not spill out over onto the top of the cake. Return to the oven for around 30 minutes until golden brown and cooked through. Remove from the oven and leave to cool in the tin. Dust with icing sugar and decorate with the fresh blueberries.

Tip: buckwheat flour
With its delicate nutty flavour, buckwheat flour is ideally suited to baking. However, due to the lack of gluten, it cannot be used as a flour substitute, but instead is simply added to cakes that get their binding properties from other ingredients.

▼

YUZU TART

with green tea and white chocolate

Serves 12   Prep: 40 mins + 28 hrs chilling + cooling   Baking time: 25–30 mins

For the ganache: 350g (12oz) white chocolate • 10g (¼oz) cocoa butter (from a health food shop)
• 350g (12oz) double cream • 10g (¼oz) liquid glucose (see p219) • 3½ tbsp yuzu sake
(from a mail order company, delicatessen, or Asian store)
For the pastry: 135g (4¾oz) unsalted butter, chopped, plus extra for the tin • 80g (2¾oz) icing sugar • 1 egg
• 2 tsp vanilla powder • seeds from ½ vanilla pod • pinch of salt • 225g (8oz) plain flour, plus extra for dusting
• 30g (1oz) ground almonds • 20g (¾oz) green tea powder (matcha, from a tea shop or Asian store)
For the crumble and decoration: 100g (3½oz) unsalted butter, chopped • 200g (7oz) plain flour
• 85g (3oz) light brown sugar • 2 tsp vanilla powder • ½ tbsp green tea powder, plus extra for decoration
• lime zest, for decoration
For the jelly: 3 leaves of gelatine • 175ml (6fl oz) yuzu sake (from a mail order company, delicatessen, or Asian store)
• 25g (scant 1oz) caster sugar
Equipment: 28cm (11in) tart tin • baking beans, dried pulses, or raw rice

1. One day in advance, chop the chocolate for the ganache finely and put it into a heatproof bowl with the cocoa butter. Put 200g (7oz) of the cream into a saucepan with the glucose and yuzu sake and bring to the boil. Pour this over the chocolate mixture and leave for 2 minutes. Then mix using a hand-held blender, gradually adding the remaining cream as you go. When doing this, try to avoid incorporating any air. Cover and refrigerate for at least 24 hours.

2. The following day prepare the pastry by kneading together the butter, icing sugar, egg, vanilla powder, vanilla seeds, and salt in the bowl of a mixer fitted with a dough hook. Add the flour, almonds, and green tea powder and work everything swiftly to a smooth consistency. Shape into a ball, press flat, wrap in cling film and refrigerate for at least 2 hours.

3. Preheat the oven to 190°C (375°F/Gas 5) and butter the tart tin. Roll out the pastry on a lightly floured work surface or between 2 sheets of cling film to a 5mm (¼in) thick circle and use this to line the tart tin. Trim off overhanging pastry and prick all over with a fork.

4. Blind-bake the pastry on the middle shelf of the preheated oven for around 10 minutes (see p59). Remove the baking beans and baking parchment and

return the tart base to the oven for 5–10 minutes until golden brown. Remove from the oven and leave to cool in the tin.

5. Meanwhile, rub all the ingredients for the crumble together with your fingertips, or using a mixer fitted with a dough hook, working until you have a crumble consistency (do not include the lime zest for decoration). Transfer to a baking tray lined with baking parchment and bake for 10 minutes.

5. Briefly beat the ganache in a bowl using an electric hand whisk on a medium setting until you have a dense, smooth consistency. Transfer the ganache to the pastry shell and smooth it out. Refrigerate for at least 1 hour.

7. To make the yuzu jelly, first soak the gelatine in cold water for 10 minutes. Briefly boil the sake with the sugar in a saucepan, then remove from the heat. Squeeze out the gelatine and dissolve it in the warmed sake mixture. Let it cool down until it is lukewarm, then carefully spread it over the tart before refrigerating for about another hour. Carefully release the tart from the tin and scatter with green tea powder, the crumble, and lime zest.

▼

MILLEFEUILLE CAKE

with plum jam

Serves 12–16   Prep: 1 hr + 30 hrs chilling + cooling   Baking time: 35 mins

Tip: size of the base
The puff pastry discs contract
slightly during baking and are,
therefore, somewhat smaller
than the shortcrust pastry base.
So the gap between the puff
pastry and the cake ring in this
recipe is filled in with cream.

For the puff pastry (basic pastry or détrempe): 40g (1¼oz) unsalted butter • 1 tsp salt • 250g (9oz) plain flour
For the puff pastry (beurrage): 160g (5¾oz) unsalted butter • 50g (1¾oz) plain flour
For the shortcrust pastry: 90g (3oz) unsalted butter • 55g (2oz) icing sugar • 1 egg, plus 1 egg yolk • pinch of salt
• seeds from ½ vanilla pod • 150g (5½oz) plain flour, plus extra for dusting • 20g (¾oz) ground almonds
For the filling and decoration: 400g (14oz) double cream • 35g (1¼oz) caster sugar • 1 tsp vanilla powder
• seeds from 1 vanilla pod • 3 sheets of gelatin • 400g (14oz) plum jam • Glacé Icing (see p219), for decoration
Equipment: 26cm (10½in) cake ring, or ring from springform tin

1. One day in advance, prepare the puff pastry (détrempe) as described (see p216).

2. The following day prepare the beurrage as described (see p216) and chill it.

3. For the shortcrust pastry, knead together the butter, icing sugar, 1 egg, salt, and vanilla seeds in the bowl of a mixer fitted with a dough hook. Add the flour and almonds and work everything swiftly to a smooth consistency. Shape into a ball, press flat, wrap in cling film, and refrigerate for at least 2 hours.

4. To finish making the puff pastry, follow the next steps for working with the détrempe and beurrage as described (see p216): namely rolling out, folding together (single and double folds), then chilling.

5. Preheat the oven to 190°C (375°F/Gas 5) and line a baking tray with baking parchment. Roll out the shortcrust pastry on a lightly floured work surface or between 2 pieces of cling film until it is 5mm (¼in) thick and stamp out a 26cm (10½in) circle using the cake ring or tin as a guide. Lay the pastry disc on the tray, prick it all over with a fork and bake it on the middle shelf of the oven for around 8 minutes until golden brown. Remove from the oven and leave to cool on a wire rack.

6. Increase the oven temperature to 220°C (425°F/ Gas 7) and line 2 baking trays with baking parchment. Roll out the puff pastry to form a large

sheet around 5mm (¼in) thick and stamp out 2 × 26cm (10½in) circles, as before. Turn the pastry circles over, lay them on the baking trays, and just brush the upper surfaces with egg yolk. No egg yolk should get onto the stamped-out edges or this will impede the rising of the puff pastry during baking. Bake the discs on the middle shelf for around 25 minutes until golden brown. Remove from the oven and leave to cool on a wire rack. Slice each of the discs in half horizontally so you get 4 layers.

7. For the filling, whip 350g (12oz) of the cream with the sugar, vanilla powder, and vanilla seeds in a bowl, using an electric hand whisk on a medium setting, until stiff. Soak the gelatin, then squeeze it. Heat the remaining 50g (2oz) of cream, dissolve the gelatin in the cream, then gradually add the cream to the whipped cream.

8. Lay the cake ring around the shortcrust pastry base and spread with 4–5 tbsp plum jam. Lay a puff pastry sheet on top of this and spread this with plum jam. Smooth one-third of the cream on top of that. Layer up another puff pastry sheet with plum jam and the remaining filling, making sure you fill right up to the edges with cream. Spread the third puff pastry sheet with plum jam and decorate with dots of glacé icing. Cut it into 12–16 portions, depending on the desired size, and lay these fanned out at a slight angle on top. (Wrap and freeze the last puff pastry circle for another occasion.) Cover and refrigerate for 4 hours. Remove the cake ring to serve.

▼

CHERRY-CHOCOLATE TARTLETS

with balsamic vinegar

For the pastry: 150g (5½oz) unsalted butter, chopped, plus extra for the tins • 100g (3½oz) icing sugar
• 1 egg • 30g (1oz) ground almonds • 250g (9oz) plain flour, plus extra for dusting
For the filling: 140g (5oz) dark chocolate (65% cocoa solids) • 100g (3½oz) double cream
• 80g (2¾oz) sour cherry purée (with 10% sugar; see p219) • 3½ tbsp matured balsamic vinegar
• 40g (1¼oz) unsalted butter, chilled • 250g (9oz) fresh sour cherries
For the crumble and decoration: 100g (3½oz) unsalted butter, chopped • 180g (6oz) plain flour • 30g (1oz)
ground hazelnuts • 85g (3oz) light brown sugar • 1½ tsp vanilla powder • milk chocolate shavings, for decoration
Equipment: 3 × 10cm (4in) tartlet tins • baking beans, dried pulses, or raw rice
• piping bag with small round nozzle

Makes 3   Prep: 40 mins + 4 hrs chilling + cooling   Baking time: 25–30 mins

1. To make the pastry, knead together the butter, icing sugar, and egg in the bowl of a mixer fitted with a dough hook. Add the almonds and flour and work swiftly until smooth. Shape the pastry into a ball, press flat, wrap in cling film, and refrigerate for at least 2 hours.

2. Preheat the oven to 180°C (350°F/Gas 4) and butter the tins. Roll out the pastry on a lightly floured work surface or between 2 pieces of cling film to a 5mm (¼in) thick circle and use this to line the tartlet tins. Trim off any overhanging pastry and prick all over with a fork.

3. Blind-bake the pastry on the middle shelf of the preheated oven for around 10 minutes, as described (see p59). Remove the baking beans and baking parchment and return the tartlet bases to the oven for 5–10 minutes until they are golden brown. Remove from the oven and leave to cool in the tin.

4. Meanwhile, finely chop the chocolate for the filling. Boil the cream with the cherry purée in a saucepan, pour it over the chocolate, and mix to a smooth consistency using a hand-held blender. Take care not to incorporate any air. Add 1–2 tsp of the balsamic vinegar, to taste. Chop the butter into little pieces and stir into the chocolate mixture.

5. Wash and pit the cherries. Divide two-thirds of the cherries between the pastry shells, then smooth over the chocolate cream filling. Gently press the remaining cherries into the cream.

6. Chill the tartlets in the refrigerator for at least 2 hours. Meanwhile, prepare and bake the crumble, as described (see p161). Just before serving, put the remaining vinegar into a piping bag fitted with a small round nozzle and squirt into the cherries protruding from the tartlets, where the pits were. Decorate with crumble and chocolate shavings.

▼

RASPBERRY HEDGEHOGS

with chocolate nougat icing

Makes 12 Prep: 1 hr + 26 hrs chilling + 3 hrs freezing + cooling Baking time: 8 mins

For the ganache: 220g (7½oz) white chocolate • 10g (¼oz) cocoa butter (from health food shops) • 400g (14oz) double cream • 10g (¼oz) liquid glucose • 230g (8oz) raspberry jam • 1½ tbsp raspberry liqueur
For the chocolate pastry: 200g (7oz) unsalted butter, chopped • 100g (3½oz) caster sugar • 1 small egg • 250g (9oz) plain flour, plus extra for dusting • 50g (1¾oz) cocoa powder
For the icing: 250g (9oz) milk chocolate • 250g (9oz) dark chocolate • 250g (9oz) nougat • 150ml (5fl oz) milk • 150g (5½oz) double cream
For the decoration: about 600g (1lb 5oz) raspberries • 200g (7oz) double cream • 1 tsp vanilla powder • milk • white chocolate shavings
Equipment: 2 × 6-hole silicone hemisphere baking moulds (each hole 6cm/2½in in diameter) • piping bag with medium round nozzle

1. One day in advance, finely chop the chocolate for the ganache and put it in a heatproof bowl with the cocoa butter. Bring 250g (9oz) of the cream to the boil with the glucose, pour over the chocolate mixture and leave for 2 minutes. Then combine with a hand-held blender, gradually working in the remaining cream as you go. When doing this, avoid incorporating any air. Cover and refrigerate for at least 24 hours.

2. The following day, make the pastry by mixing the butter, sugar, and egg in the bowl of a mixer fitted with a dough hook. Add the flour and cocoa powder and swiftly work everything to a smooth consistency. Shape into a ball, press it flat, wrap in cling film, and refrigerate for around 2 hours.

3. Preheat the oven to 190°C (375°F/Gas 5) and line a baking tray with baking parchment. Roll out the shortcrust pastry on a lightly floured work surface or between 2 sheets of cling film until it is about 5mm (¼in) thick, then use a cutter or a glass to stamp out 12 × 6cm (2½in) circles. Lay the pastry circles on the baking tray and bake on the middle shelf of the preheated oven for around 8 minutes until golden brown. Remove from the oven and leave to cool on a wire rack.

4. Beat the ganache very briefly using an electric hand whisk on a medium setting and stir in the raspberry jam and liqueur to produce a dense, smooth mixture. Fill the silicone moulds with the ganache and top each with a pastry circle. Transfer them to the freezer and leave for around 3 hours.

5. To make the chocolate icing, finely chop both types of chocolate and the nougat. Bring the milk and cream to the boil in a saucepan, stir in the chocolate and leave to melt. Mix in the nougat using a hand-held blender, taking care not to incorporate any air. Leave to cool slightly.

6. To assemble the hedgehogs, put a wire rack on a baking tray or piece of baking parchment. Slip the frozen cakes out of the silicone moulds, put them on the rack and cover with the warm icing. Add the raspberries (open ends facing down) sticking them all over until each little cake is completely covered. Whip the cream and vanilla powder in a bowl until stiff using an electric hand whisk on a medium setting, spoon into a piping bag fitted with a round nozzle, and pipe little blobs in the gaps between the berries. Decorate with chocolate shavings.

▼

APRICOT CAKE

with buckwheat and lemon verbena

For the topping: **500g (1lb 2oz) apricots** • **5 lemon verbena leaves (see tip)** • **100g (3½oz) caster sugar**
For the cake: **310g (10½oz) unsalted butter, plus extra for the tin** • **100g (3½oz) buckwheat flour, plus extra for the tin**
• **210g (7½oz) caster sugar** • **5 eggs** • **130g (4¾oz) plain flour** • **1 tsp baking powder** • **100g (3½oz) soured cream**
For the glaze and decoration: **4 tbsp apricot jam** • **lemon verbena leaves, for decoration** • **icing sugar, for dusting**
Equipment: **28cm (11in) springform tin**

Serves 16   Prep: 30 mins + 24 hrs marinating + cooling   Baking time: 50 mins

1. One day in advance, prepare the apricots for the topping: halve them and remove the stones. Put the lemon verbena into a saucepan with 100ml (3½fl oz) of water and the sugar and bring to the boil. Add the apricots, cool, cover, and refrigerate for 24 hours.

2. The following day, preheat the oven to 180°C (350°F/Gas 4). Butter the tin and sprinkle with buckwheat flour, knocking out any excess.

3. Cream the butter with the sugar. Gradually mix in the eggs. Combine the flour, buckwheat flour, and baking powder. Stir the soured cream into the butter and egg mixture and finally fold in the flour mixture.

4. Spoon into the tin and bake on the middle shelf of the preheated oven for around 50 minutes until golden brown. Leave to cool in the tin.

5. Drain the marinated apricot halves and spread them over the cake. Warm the jam in a small saucepan, then press through a sieve. Brush the apricots with the glaze. Decorate with lemon verbena leaves and dust with icing sugar.

Tip: a fresh citrus-fragrant herb
Lemon verbena has a pleasant, fruity citrus aroma and so is absolutely ideal for summery cakes or drinks. You can buy the seeds, or the herb itself in pots from garden centres, to grow in a window box or in the garden. Alternatively, you could also use lemon balm for this recipe.

▼

MASTER BAKING TO IMPRESS

Macarons, cronuts, millefeuille, or vanilla crème brûlée tart; these are recipes which will truly wow your guests. Needless to say, if you can rustle up one of these dishes, you will have earned an Oscar for baking!

▼

MACARONS

with chocolate or nougat filling

For the macarons: 300g (10oz) tant pour tant (see p179) • 300g (10oz) icing sugar • 50g (1¾oz) cocoa powder • 220g (8oz) egg white (from a carton, or from about 6 eggs) • a little chocolate brown food colouring, liquid or powder (only for the macarons with chocolate filling) • 340g (11½oz) caster sugar

For the chocolate ganache (for 50 macarons): 75g (2½oz) dark chocolate (70% cocoa solids) • 100g (3½oz) milk chocolate • 100g (3½oz) double cream • 30g (1oz) liquid glucose (see p219) • 2 tbsp Baileys • 30g (1oz) unsalted butter

For the nougat ganache (for 50 macarons): 50g (1¾oz) milk chocolate • 100g (3½oz) nougat • 100g (3½oz) double cream • 2 tbsp liquid glucose (see p219) • 2 tbsp Baileys • 30g (1oz) unsalted butter

Equipment: sugar thermometer or kitchen thermometer • reusable silicone baking paper or silicone baking mat • piping bag with round 6mm and 8mm (¼ and ⅓in) nozzles

Makes about 50   Prep: 1 hr + 24 hrs chilling   Baking time: 30 mins

1. To make the macarons, combine the tant pour tant with the icing sugar and cocoa powder in the bowl of a mixer fitted with a dough hook. Add 110g (3¾oz) of the egg white and mix thoroughly until you have a mixture that resembles marzipan. For the macarons with chocolate filling, add a few drops of chocolate brown food colouring and work this into the mixture to produce a strong chocolate colour (if you are using food colouring powder, first mix it with as little water as possible). If the mixture is still very stiff, knead it a bit longer until it is softer.

2. Whisk the remaining egg white with 40g (1¼oz) of the caster sugar in the mixer fitted with a whisk, on a medium setting, until they are just holding their shape, then turn the machine off. Heat the remaining sugar in a saucepan with 100ml (3½fl oz) of water to 113°C (235°F), monitoring the temperature with a sugar or kitchen thermometer.

3. Switch the mixer with the semi-stiff beaten egg whites on to a medium setting once more and slowly pour in the hot sugar syrup in a thin stream. Switch the mixture to medium-high and beat until cold.

4. Put one-third of the whipped egg white mixture into the bowl with the almond mixture and work it in using a spatula until you have a smooth consistency. Then fold in the remaining beaten egg whites in the same way until you have a smooth mixture which can be piped.

5. Preheat the oven to 140°C (275°F/Gas 1), without the fan, and line 2 baking trays with reusable silicone baking paper or a silicone baking mat. Transfer the macaron mixture into a piping bag fitted with a 6mm (¼in) round nozzle and pipe 4cm (1½in) diameter, 5mm (¼in) high circles, 1–2 cm (½–¾in) apart, onto the baking trays. Let the macaron mixture dry out a little until it is no longer sticky to the touch and has formed a skin.

6. Swiftly put a tray of macarons on the middle shelf of the preheated oven so that this doesn't cool down. Bake for around 15 minutes. They are ready when they have formed a nice base and a firm crust. Remove from the oven and leave to cool on a wire rack. Bake the macarons on the second baking tray in the same way. Leave to cool. Store at room temperature in an airtight container until ready for the next step.

7. To make the chocolate ganache, finely chop the dark and milk chocolates and put them into a heatproof bowl. Bring the cream to the boil in a saucepan with the glucose and pour this over the chocolate, stirring everything into a glossy mixture. Stir in the Baileys. Chop the butter into little pieces and work this in using a hand-held blender. Cover with cling film and refrigerate for at least 24 hours.

8. To make the nougat ganache, finely chop the milk chocolate and nougat into pieces and put both in a heatproof bowl. Bring the cream to the boil in a pan with the glucose and pour this over the chopped chocolate and nougat, stirring everything into a glossy mixture. Stir in the Baileys. Chop the butter into little pieces and work this in using a hand-held blender. Cover with cling film and refrigerate for at least 24 hours.

9. To fill the macarons, remove the ganache from the refrigerator 30 minutes before use to return it to room temperature. Then spoon it into a piping bag fitted with an 8mm (⅓in) round nozzle. Pipe some ganache onto the lower section of a macaron and carefully press a second macaron flat-side down on top of this.

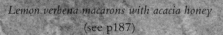

Lemon verbena macarons with acacia honey
(see p187)

Macarons with raspberry ganache
(see p176)

Macarons with nougat filling
(see p172)

Blueberry macarons with sesame
(see p186)

The artist has his palette of colours and the pâtissier
has the flavours he works with, which he can draw on
to create his works of art.

Matcha macarons with passion fruit
(see p180)

Macarons with chocolate filling
(see p192)

Lychee macarons with green tea
(see p182)

▼

MACARONS

with raspberry ganache

For the macarons: 350g (12oz) tant pour tant (see p179) • 350g (12oz) icing sugar • 220g (8oz) egg white (from a carton, or from about 6 eggs) • a little red food colouring, liquid or powder • 340g (11½oz) caster sugar
For the raspberry ganache: 190g (6½oz) white chocolate • 150g (5½oz) raspberry purée (with 10% sugar, see p219)
• 100g (3½oz) caster sugar • 20g (¾oz) liquid glucose (see p219) • 20g (¾oz) raspberry powder (see p219)
• 10g (¼oz) vitamin C powder (ascorbic acid, from a pharmacy) • 125g (4½oz) unsalted butter, chilled
Equipment: sugar thermometer or kitchen thermometer • reusable silicone baking paper or silicone baking mat
• piping bag with round 6mm and 8mm (¼in and ⅓in) nozzles

Makes about 50   Prep: 1 hr + 24 hrs chilling   Baking time: 30 mins

1. Prepare the macarons from the tant pour tant, icing sugar, egg white, food colouring, and caster sugar, as described (see p173).

2. To make the raspberry ganache, chop the chocolate finely and melt it in a heatproof bowl over simmering water (don't let the bowl touch the water). Put the raspberry purée into a saucepan with the sugar, glucose, raspberry powder, and vitamin C powder, and heat to around 90°C (194°F).

3. Stir the chocolate into the raspberry mixture until it has melted. Chop the cold butter into little pieces and use a hand-held blender to work this into the chocolate mixture. Take care when doing this not to incorporate any air. Cover and refrigerate for at least 24 hours.

4. To fill the macarons, remove the ganache from the refrigerator 30 minutes before use to return it to room temperature. Then spoon it into a piping bag fitted with an 8mm (⅓in) round nozzle. Pipe some ganache onto the lower section of a macaron and carefully press a second macaron flat-side down on top of this.

Tip: build in little surprises
If you fancy surprising your guests, just pipe a ring of ganache onto the lower section of each macaron, leaving the centre free. In this hole you can put half a fresh raspberry before carefully positioning the lid on top. This also tastes great in Macarons with chocolate filling (see p172).

▼

MACARONS

with cassis ganache

For the macarons: 350g (12oz) tant pour tant (see p179) • 350g (12oz) icing sugar • 220g (8oz) egg white (from a carton, or from about 6 eggs) • a little violet food colouring, liquid or powder • 340g (11½oz) caster sugar
For the cassis ganache: 150g (5½oz) blackcurrant purée (with 10% sugar, see p219)
• 120g (4fl oz) extra thick double cream • 30g (1oz) blackcurrant powder (see p219)
• 1½ tbsp crème de cassis • seeds from ½ vanilla pod • 200g (7oz) white chocolate
• 130g (4¾oz) unsalted butter, chilled • vitamin C powder, to taste (ascorbic acid, from a pharmacy)
Equipment: sugar thermometer or kitchen thermometer • reusable silicone baking paper or silicone baking mat
• piping bag with round 6mm and 8mm (¼in and ⅓in) nozzles

Makes about 50   Prep: 1 hr + 24 hrs chilling   Baking time: 30 mins

1. Prepare the macarons from the tant pour tant, icing sugar, egg white, food colouring, and caster sugar, as described (see p173).

2. To make the cassis ganache, heat the blackcurrant purée in a pan with the extra thick double cream, blackcurrant powder, crème de cassis, and vanilla seeds, but do not let it boil. Finely chop the chocolate and melt it in a heatproof bowl over simmering water (don't let the bowl touch the water).

3. Pour the chocolate into the warm blackcurrant mixture and stir everything with a wooden spoon until you have a glossy mixture. Chop the butter into little pieces and use a hand-held blender to work it into the chocolate mixture, incorporating as little air as possible. Add vitamin C powder to the mixture to taste, cover and refrigerater for at least 24 hours.

4. To fill the macarons, remove the ganache from the refrigerator 30 minutes before use to return it to room temperature. Then spoon it into a piping bag fitted with an 8mm (⅓in) round nozzle. Pipe some ganache onto the lower section of a macaron and carefully press a second macaron flat-side down on top of this.

Tip: macarons with passion fruit ganache
You can create macarons with a passion fruit ganache in the same way, by substituting passion fruit purée and passion fruit powder for the blackcurrant varieties. You can leave out the crème de cassis, as passion fruit purée is more liquid than blackcurrant purée.

▼

MACARONS

These little almond meringue discs are regarded by many as the
supreme discipline in French pâtisserie. In Paris, there are countless
pâtissiers who compete to produce the finest macarons in the city.

Lemon verbena
macarons
(see p187)

Matcha macarons
(see p180)

Raspberry macarons
(see p176)

(see p176)

Tip: tant pour tant
The quality of macarons stands or falls by the quality of the 'tant pour tant' used in the mixture. It is a mixture of ground almonds and icing sugar. For the finest result, don't try to make tant pour tant yourself; instead, buy it from an online retailer (see p218).

▼

MATCHA MACARONS

with passion fruit

For the macarons: 350g (12oz) tant pour tant (see p179) • 350g (12oz) icing sugar • 220g (8oz) egg white (from a carton, or from about 6 eggs) • a little green food colouring, liquid or powder • 340g (11½oz) caster sugar
For the matcha and passion fruit ganache: 300g (10oz) white chocolate • 100g (3½oz) passion fruit purée (with 10% sugar; see p219) • 20g (¾oz) green tea powder (matcha, from a tea shop or Asian store) • 10g (¼oz) liquid glucose • 25g (scant 1oz) extra thick double cream
Equipment: sugar thermometer or kitchen thermometer • reusable silicone baking paper or silicone baking mat • piping bag with round 6mm and 8mm (¼ and ⅓in) nozzles

Makes about 50   Prep: 1 hr + 24 hrs chilling   Baking time: 30 mins

For around 12 years my work has involved macarons and I have come to be almost obsessed by France's number one national pâtisserie. I've spent a lot of time working on the perfect macaron, because success is dependent on so many different factors: from the ambient temperature to the baking temperature to the temperature of the sugar… or indeed the humidity. For this book I have selected only my very finest creations and this is one example: the strong grassy notes of the green tea are combined with the floral acidity of passion fruit.

1. Prepare and bake the macarons from the tant pour tant, icing sugar, egg white, food colouring, and caster sugar, as described (see p173).

2. To make the ganache, finely chop the chocolate and put it in a heatproof bowl. Put the passion fruit purée into a saucepan with the green tea powder, glucose, and the extra thick double cream, and bring to the boil. Pour this over the chocolate in the bowl and leave for 2 minutes. Then use a hand-held blender to mix everything until smooth. Cover and refrigerate for at least 24 hours.

3. To fill the macarons, remove the ganache from the refrigerator 30 minutes before use to return it to room temperature. Then spoon it into a piping bag fitted with an 8mm (⅓in) round nozzle. Pipe some ganache onto the lower section of a macaron and carefully press a second macaron flat-side down on top of this.

▼

CARAMEL MACARONS

with fleur de sel

For the macarons: **320g (11oz) tant pour tant (see p179)** • **320g (11oz) icing sugar** • **10g (¼oz) cocoa powder**
• **220g (8oz) egg white (from a carton, or from about 6 eggs)** • **340g (11½oz) caster sugar**
For the caramel ganache: **60g (2oz) caster sugar** • **115g (4oz) double cream** • **185g (6½oz) milk chocolate**
• **20g (¾oz) cocoa butter (from a health food shop)** • **100g (3½oz) unsalted butter, chilled**
• **sea salt flakes, ideally fleur de sel, to taste**
Equipment: **sugar thermometer or kitchen thermometer** • **reusable silicone baking paper or silicone baking mat**
• **piping bag with round 6mm and 8mm (¼ and ⅓in) nozzles**

Makes about 50   Prep: 1 hr + 24 hrs chilling   Baking time: 30 mins

For a refined, nuanced flavour, sprinkle a couple more flakes of fleur de sel on the ganache when you fill
the macarons. Let them stand for a few hours between filling and serving, to help the flavours develop.

1. Prepare and bake the macarons from the tant pour tant, icing sugar, cocoa powder, egg white, and caster sugar, as described (see p173).

2. To make the ganache, boil the sugar with 2 tbsp of water in a saucepan over a medium heat until you have a dark caramel. Add the cream and boil until the caramel dissolves. Leave to cool down slightly.

3. Finely chop the chocolate and melt it with the cocoa butter in a heatproof bowl over simmering water (don't let the bowl touch the water). Stir it into the caramel. Chop the butter and work it in using a hand-held blender. Add a pinch of salt to taste. Cover with cling film and refrigerate for 24 hours.

4. To fill the macarons, remove the ganache from the refrigerator 30 minutes before use to return it to room temperature. Then spoon it into a piping bag fitted with an 8mm (⅓in) round nozzle. Pipe some ganache onto the lower section of a macaron and carefully press a second macaron flat-side down on top of this.

▼

LYCHEE MACARONS

with green tea

For the macarons: 325g (11oz) tant pour tant (see p179) • 325g (11oz) icing sugar • 220g (8oz) egg white (from a carton, or from about 6 eggs) • 340g (11½oz) caster sugar
For the lychee and green tea ganache: 450g (1lb) white chocolate • 3 leaves of gelatine • 230g (8oz) lychee purée (with 10% sugar; see p219) • 200g (7oz) extra thick double cream • 6 egg yolks • 1 tsp vitamin C powder (ascorbic acid, from a pharmacy) • 6g green tea powder (matcha, from a tea shop or Asian store) • 100g (3½oz) unsalted butter, chilled
Equipment: sugar thermometer or kitchen thermometer • reusable silicone baking paper or silicone baking mat
• piping bag with round 6mm and 8mm (¼ and ⅓in) nozzles

Makes about 50   Prep: 1 hr + 24 hrs chilling   Baking time: 30 mins

1. Prepare the macarons from the tant pour tant, icing sugar, egg white, and caster sugar, as described (see p173).

2. To make the ganache, finely chop the chocolate. Soak the gelatine in cold water for 10 minutes. Heat the lychee purée with the extra thick double cream, egg yolks, and vitamin C powder in a saucepan, stirring constantly until it reaches 85°C (185°F), using a kitchen thermometer.

3. Squeeze out the gelatine and add it to the warmed lychee mixture with the green tea powder, stirring

until the gelatine dissolves. Mix in the chocolate using a hand-held blender until it melts. Chop the butter into little pieces and likewise work this into the mixture. Cover with cling film and refrigerate for at least 24 hours.

4. To fill the macarons, remove the ganache from the refrigerator 30 minutes before use to return to room temperature. Then spoon it into a piping bag fitted with an 8mm (⅓in) round nozzle. Pipe some ganache onto the lower section of a macaron and carefully press a second macaron flat-side down on top of this.

Nougat macarons
(see p192)

Lychee macarons
(see left)

Chocolate macarons
(see p172)

Blueberry macarons
(see p186)

Lychee macarons
(see p182)

Tip: achieving great ganache
When making a ganache or
cream filling, once all the
ingredients have been combined,
let the mixture cool to 40–45 °C
(104–113°F), monitoring the
temperature with a kitchen
thermometer, then emulsify
it thoroughly again using a
hand-held blender. If the
temperature is still too high, this
may cause the butter to separate
out. (Water and fat molecules
can't combine properly in these
conditions and you won't get a
smooth ganache.)

▼

BLUEBERRY MACARONS

with sesame

For the macarons: 350g (12oz) tant pour tant (see p179) • 350g (12oz) icing sugar • 220g (8oz) egg white
(from a carton, or from about 6 eggs) • a little dark blue food colouring, liquid or powder • 340g (11½oz) caster sugar
For the blueberry and sesame ganache: 350g (12oz) white chocolate • 225g (8oz) blueberry purée (with 10% sugar;
see p219) • 180g (6oz) extra thick double cream • 1 tsp vitamin C powder (ascorbic acid; from a pharmacy)
• 10g (¼oz) blackcurrant powder (see p219) • 1 tbsp toasted sesame oil • 200g (7oz) unsalted butter, chilled
Equipment: sugar thermometer or kitchen thermometer • reusable silicone baking paper or silicone baking mat
• piping bag with round 6mm and 8mm (¼ and ⅓in) nozzles

Makes about 50   Prep: 1 hr + 24 hrs chilling   Baking time: 30 mins

1. Prepare the macarons from the tant pour tant, icing sugar, egg white, food colouring, and caster sugar, as described (see p173).

2. To make the blueberry and sesame ganache, finely chop the chocolate and put it in a heatproof bowl. Put the blueberry purée in a saucepan with the extra thick double cream, vitamin C powder, blackcurrant powder, and sesame oil, and bring briefly to the boil. Pour this over the chocolate and leave for 2 minutes.

3. Use a hand-held blender to blend the chocolate mixture to a smooth consistency. Chop the butter into little pieces and work these into the mixture. Cover and refrigerate for at least 24 hours.

4. To fill the macarons, remove the ganache from the refrigerator 30 minutes before use to return it to room temperature. Then spoon it into a piping bag fitted with an 8mm (⅓in) round nozzle. Pipe some ganache onto the lower section of a macaron and carefully press a second macaron flat-side down on top of this.

Tip: a touch of colour
The blue macaron discs and the rich dark purple berry notes of the blueberry and sesame ganache look particularly cool because they contrast so fantastically (see p184). Truly eye catching.

▼

LEMON VERBENA MACARONS

with acacia honey

For the macarons: 350g (12oz) tant pour tant (see p179) • 350g (12oz) icing sugar • 220g (8oz) egg white (from a carton, or about 6 eggs) • a little lemon yellow food colouring, liquid or powder • 340g (11½oz) caster sugar
For the lemon verbena cream filling: 100ml (3½fl oz) milk • 75g (2½oz) extra thick double cream • 3 bunches of lemon verbena • 400g (14oz) white chocolate • 3 leaves of gelatine • 50g (1¾oz) caster sugar • 25g (scant 1oz) acacia honey • 6 egg yolks • 100g (3½oz) unsalted butter, chilled
Equipment: sugar thermometer or kitchen thermometer • reusable silicone baking paper or silicone baking mat • piping bag with round 6mm and 8mm (¼ and ⅓in) nozzles

Makes about 50   Prep: 1 hr + 24 hrs chilling   Baking time: 30 mins

1. Prepare the macarons from the tant pour tant, icing sugar, egg white, food colouring, and caster sugar, as described (see p173).

2. To make the lemon verbena cream filling, bring the milk to the boil in a saucepan with the extra thick double cream. Remove from the heat, add the lemon verbena, cover, and leave to infuse in the refrigerator for at least 4 hours.

3. Finely chop the chocolate and put it in a heatproof bowl. Soak the gelatine in cold water for 10 minutes. Strain the lemon verbena mixture through a fine sieve into a saucepan. Add the sugar, honey, and egg yolks, and heat the mixture, stirring constantly until it reaches 85°C (185°F), using a thermometer.

4. Remove the pan from the heat, squeeze out the gelatine and dissolve it in the warmed cream. Pour over the chocolate and combine everything to a smooth consistency using a hand-held blender. Chop the butter into little pieces and work this into the mixture. Cover and refrigerate the cream filling for at least 24 hours.

5. To fill the macarons, remove the ganache from the refrigerator 30 minutes before use to return it to room temperature. Then spoon it into a piping bag fitted with an 8mm (⅓in) round nozzle. Pipe some ganache onto the lower section of a macaron and carefully press a second macaron flat-side down on top of this.

▼

CARROT AND MASCARPONE CUPCAKES

with chocolate soil

Makes 12   Prep: 30 mins + 1 hr chilling + cooling   Baking time: 35 mins

For the cakes: 150ml (5fl oz) flavourless vegetable oil, plus extra for the moulds (optional) • 2 carrots, about 250g (9oz) in total • 220g (8oz) plain flour • 1 tsp baking powder • 1 tsp bicarbonate of soda • ½ tsp ground cinnamon • small pinch of freshly grated nutmeg • 20g (¾oz) walnuts, chopped • 150g (5½oz) caster sugar • 2 eggs • finely grated zest of ½ orange • pinch of salt

For the chocolate soil: 100g (3½oz) light brown sugar • 200g (7oz) plain flour • 20g (¾oz) rye flour • 40g (1¼oz) cocoa powder • 40g (1¼oz) ground almonds • 100g (3½oz) unsalted butter, chopped

For the mascarpone cream: 1½ leaves of gelatine • 125g (4½oz) double cream • 250g (9oz) mascarpone • 25g (scant 1oz) caster sugar • 2 tbsp almond syrup (such as from Monin)

For decoration: finely grated orange zest (optional) • walnuts, chopped and caramelized (see p43) • little carrots, in freshly shaved slices (ideally including some of the green tops)

Equipment: 12-hole muffin tray • 12 paper muffin cases (optional) • piping bag with large round or star nozzle

1. Preheat the oven to 180°C (350°F/Gas 4). Oil the muffin moulds, or insert a paper case into each.

2. Peel and finely grate the carrots. Mix together the flour, baking powder, bicarbonate of soda, cinnamon, nutmeg, and walnuts. Beat the sugar with the eggs, orange zest, and salt in a bowl for around 10 minutes using an electric hand whisk on a medium setting. Gradually stir in the oil and continue blending for a couple of minutes. Fold in the carrots, and then the flour mixture.

3. Spoon the batter evenly between the moulds or cases. Bake on the middle shelf of the preheated oven for around 25 minutes. Remove from the oven and leave to cool in the tray. Increase the oven temperature to 190°C (375°F/Gas 5).

4. Mix all the ingredients for the chocolate soil in a bowl and work to a crumble with your fingertips or in a mixer fitted with a dough hook. Spread on a baking tray lined with baking parchment. Bake in the preheated oven for 10 minutes. Leave to cool.

5. Meanwhile, soak the gelatine for the mascarpone cream in cold water for 10 minutes. Whip the cream in bowl using an electric hand whisk until it is just holding its shape. Stir the mascarpone together with the sugar in a bowl. Gently heat the almond syrup in a pan, squeeze out the gelatine and dissolve it in the warmed syrup. Stir about 2 tbsp of the mascarpone mixture into the syrup mixture in the pan, then swiftly stir this into the remaining mascarpone cream using a balloon whisk. Finally, carefully fold in the cream. Cover and refrigerate for about 1 hour to let the cream set.

6. To assemble the cupcakes, stir the mascarpone cream with the balloon whisk and spoon it into a piping bag fitted with a round or star nozzle. Pipe some of the cream onto each cupcake and decorate with the chocolate soil, orange zest (if using), caramelized walnuts, and strips of carrot.

▼

CRONUTS

with praline cream filling and caramelized hazelnuts

For the puff pastry (yeasted dough) and for frying and decoration: 500g (1lb 2oz) plain flour, plus extra for dusting
• ½ tsp salt • 200ml (7fl oz) milk • 70g (2¼oz) caster sugar • 30g (1oz) fresh yeast • 1 egg • 30g (1oz) unsalted butter,
at room temperature • 2 litres (3½ pints) flavourless vegetable oil, for frying • poured fondant or glacé icing
(optional, see p219) • milk chocolate shavings

For the puff pastry (beurrage): 400g (14oz) unsalted butter • 120g (4¼oz) plain flour

For the caramelized hazelnuts: 200g (7oz) caster sugar • 300g (10oz) blanched hazelnuts
• 180ml (6fl oz) flavourless vegetable oil • sea salt flakes, to taste

For the hazelnut cream: 65g (2¼oz) caster sugar • 3 small egg yolks • 25g (scant 1oz) vanilla blancmange mix
• ½ vanilla pod • 250ml (9fl oz) milk • 250g (9oz) hazelnut praline paste (60% hazelnut, see p218)

Equipment: 8cm (3in) round doughnut cutter, or 4cm (1½in) and 8cm (3in) round cutters
• kitchen thermometer (optional) • piping bag with filler nozzle or medium round nozzle

Makes about 10   Prep: 70 mins + 3 hrs resting + 40 mins frying + chilling

1. Prepare the yeasted dough and beurrage for the cronuts, as described (see p217), and leave to prove or chill, as appropriate.

2. Meanwhile, get a large piece of baking parchment ready for the caramelized hazelnuts. Boil the sugar and 200ml (7fl oz) of water in a saucepan until the sugar has dissolved. Warm a non-stick saucepan over a medium heat, add the hazelnuts and shake the pan until the nuts are golden brown. Add the sugar syrup to the nuts and heat while continuously agitating the pan, until the sugar has become more viscous but has not yet darkened in colour. Add the oil so the nuts are swimming in it and continue to cook the nuts while agitating the pan until they have caramelized to a golden brown. Pour the nuts into a fine sieve and let them drain briefly before immediately spreading them out on the prepared baking parchment and using a spoon to separate them from each other. Leave the nuts to cool. If you like, you can also sprinkle 1–2 pinches of sea salt flakes over the still-warm nuts.

3. To make the hazelnut cream, stir one-third of the sugar with the egg yolks and vanilla blancmange mix in a bowl. Cut the vanilla pod in half lengthways and scrape out the seeds with a knife. Add the vanilla seeds and pod to the milk and the remaining sugar in a saucepan and bring to the boil, stirring constantly. Remove the vanilla pod and pour the hot milk over the egg yolk mixture, whisking all the time with a balloon whisk. Return the mixture to the saucepan and return briefly to the boil to thicken. Then transfer immediately to a cold container and leave to cool, covered with cling film.

4. Combine the praline paste and the cream mixture in a bowl by stirring thoroughly with the balloon whisk. Put half the caramelized hazelnuts into a freezer bag and crush with a rolling pin or saucepan, use the remaining whole nuts for decoration. Mix the crushed nuts into the cream, cover, and refrigerate until ready for use.

5. Continue the next steps for the yeasted dough and the beurrage, as described (see p217): namely rolling out, folding together (single and double folds), and chilling as specified. Then roll out the dough to form a 3–4cm (1¼–1½in) thick sheet and use the cutter or cutters to stamp out rings. Turn the rings over, cover, and leave to rest for 10 minutes in the refrigerator.

6. Meanwhile, heat the oil for frying in a high-sided pan to 180°C (350°F), and keep the temperature stable. Use a kitchen thermometer, or hold a wooden spoon handle in the oil: the oil is hot enough when tiny bubbles rise up it. Cook the dough rings carefully, in batches, in the hot oil for 4 minutes on both sides until golden brown, turning with a slotted spoon. Remove with a slotted spoon, let them drain, and lay them on kitchen paper to blot off the oil.

7. To assemble, either pipe in the cream using a piping bag fitted with a filler nozzle, or slice the cronuts in half horizontally and pipe some of the hazelnut cream onto the lower half of each ring using a piping bag fitted with a round nozzle before replacing the upper section. If you like you can ice the cronuts with poured fondant or glacé icing (which should be at a lukewarm temperature). Decorate with a few caramelized hazelnuts and milk chocolate shavings.

Tip: particularly light hazelnut cream
The cream will be even lighter if you fold in around 200g (7oz) whipped double cream.

Tip: cronuts with caramel sauce
To make a caramel sauce, put 200g (7oz) caster sugar in a saucepan with 3½ tbsp of water and boil until you have a dark caramel. Add 200g (7oz) extra thick double cream and continue to cook until you have a smooth consistency. Add a pinch of sea salt and leave to cool. Use the sauce to decorate, or as an additional filling for the cronuts.

▼

MILLEFEUILLE PASTRIES

with berries and vanilla cream

Makes about 10   Prep: 30 mins + 26 hrs chilling + cooling   Baking time: 10–15 mins

For the puff pastry (basic pastry or détrempe): 40g (1¼oz) unsalted butter, plus extra for the tray, plus extra, melted, to caramelize • 1 tsp salt • 250g (9oz) plain flour
For the puff pastry (beurrage): 160g (5¾oz) unsalted butter • 50g (1¾oz) plain flour
For the vanilla cream and berries: 250ml (9fl oz) milk • 250g (9oz) double cream • seeds from 1 vanilla pod • 75g (2½oz) caster sugar, plus extra to caramelize • 5 egg yolks • 1 sachet of vanilla blancmange mix • 300g (10oz) berries, such as strawberries, blueberries, raspberries, blackberries, or blackcurrants
In addition: piping bag with medium round nozzle • cook's blowtorch (optional)

1. One day in advance, prepare the puff pastry (détrempe), as described (see p216).

2. The following day, prepare the beurrage (see p216) and chill it.

3. Meanwhile, make the vanilla cream: put the milk into a saucepan with the cream, vanilla seeds, and sugar, and bring to the boil. Stir the egg yolks and blancmange mix together in a bowl. Gradually pour the hot milk over the egg yolk mixture, stirring constantly. Return the whole thing to the pan and return to the boil until it thickens. Push through a fine sieve, cover the surface with cling film and allow to cool before refrigerating.

4. To finish making the puff pastry, follow the next steps for working with the détrempe and beurrage, as described (see p216): rolling out, folding together (single and double folds), then chilling as specified.

5. Preheat the oven to 220°C (425°F/Gas 7). Roll out the puff pastry to form an 8mm (⅓in) thick rectangle. Use a sharp knife to cut into 10 × 5cm (4 × 2in) rectangles. Turn the pastry pieces over, lay them on a buttered baking tray and bake on the middle shelf of the preheated oven for 10–15 minutes until golden brown. Remove from the tray and cool on a wire rack. Slice each twice horizontally so each millefeuille pastry will have 3 layers.

6. Transfer the vanilla cream into a piping bag fitted with a round nozzle. For each millefeuille pastry, first pipe blobs of vanilla cream onto the lower pastry rectangle, leaving gaps in between. In the gaps, place some berries. Lay the middle pastry rectangle on top and cover with vanilla cream and berries in an identical manner. The top layer consists of a caramelized puff pastry rectangle. To do this, brush the surface of the remaining pastry rectangles with some melted butter and press into some sugar. Caramelize with a cook's blowtorch, or heat a frying pan and lay the pastry rectangles in it sugar-side down to caramelize over a medium heat. Lay each, caramelized-side up, on the millefeuilles.

Tip: perfect puff pastry
By repeatedly folding and rolling out the pastry, you get alternating layers of pastry and butter. The butter layers ensure that, when the pastry is later baked, the thin pastry layers separate nicely from each other. In order for the puff pastry to succeed it is very important that no butter escapes from the pastry when you are rolling it out. For this reason it is vital to adhere to the chilling times specified between rolling out, so that the butter is always sufficiently firm.

▼

CRÈME BRÛLÉE TART

with vanilla

For the pastry: 150g (5½oz) unsalted butter, chopped, plus extra for the tin • 100g (3½oz) icing sugar • 1 egg
• 30g (1oz) ground almonds • 250g (9oz) plain flour, plus extra for dusting
For the crème brûlée: 500g (1lb 2oz) double cream • 100ml (3½fl oz) milk • 80g (2¾oz) caster sugar,
plus extra for caramelizing • seeds from 2 vanilla pods • 8 egg yolks
In addition: 24cm (9½in) tart tin • baking beans, dried pulses, or raw rice • cook's blow torch

Serves 12   Prep: 30 mins + 2 hrs chilling + cooling   Baking time: 2 hrs

1. To make the shortcrust pastry, knead the butter, icing sugar, and egg in the bowl of a mixer fitted with a dough hook. Add the almonds and the flour and work swiftly to a smooth consistency. Shape the pastry into a ball, press flat, wrap in cling film, and refrigerate for at least 2 hours.

2. Preheat the oven to 180°C (350°F/Gas 4) and butter the tin. Roll out the pastry on a lightly floured work surface or between 2 sheets of cling film to a roughly 5mm (¼in) thick circle and use this to line the tart tin. Trim off any overhanging pastry edges and prick all over with a fork.

3. To blind-bake the pastry, line with baking parchment and fill with baking beans to weigh it down. Bake on the middle shelf of the hot oven for 8–10 minutes. Take the tart out of the oven and remove the baking beans and parchment. Reduce the oven temperature to 100°C (212°C/Gas ¼).

4. For the crème brûlée filling, put the cream in a saucepan with the milk, sugar, and vanilla seeds and bring to the boil. Meanwhile, whisk the egg yolks thoroughly in a bowl with a balloon whisk. Pour the hot cream and milk mixture over the egg yolks, stirring constantly with the balloon whisk.

5. Pour the crème brûlée filling into the pastry case; the filling should come up to just below the rim. Return to the oven and finish baking for around 80–110 minutes until the filling has set. Remove from the oven and leave to cool in the tin.

6. Shortly before serving, sprinkle a thin layer of sugar over the tart and use a cook's blow torch to caramelize it to a golden brown colour.

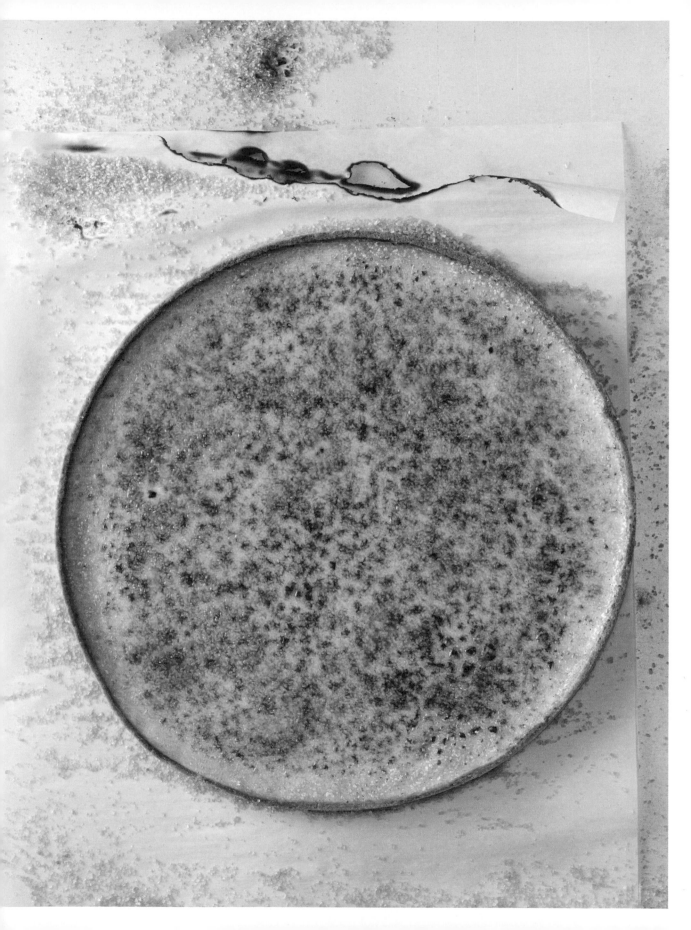

▼

PASSION FRUIT TARTLETS

exotic and delicious

Makes 8–10
Prep: 40 mins + 4 hrs chilling + cooling
Baking time: 15–20 mins

Tip: try decorating with passion fruit seeds
For decorating, use 1 extra fresh passion fruit. Cut the fruit in half and spread the flesh – including the seeds – over the not-yet-completely-set passion fruit jelly. Then leave the jelly to set completely.

For the pastry and chocolate: 150g (5½oz) unsalted butter, chopped, plus extra for the tins • 100g (3½oz) icing sugar • 1 egg • 30g (1oz) ground almonds • 250g (9oz) plain flour, plus extra for dusting • 100g (3½oz) white chocolate
For the filling: 4 large eggs • 250g (9oz) caster sugar • 50g (1¾oz) vanilla blancmange mix • 4 leaves of gelatine • 300ml (½ pint) milk • 200g (7oz) passion fruit purée (with 10% sugar, see p219) • 200g (7oz) unsalted butter • seeds from 1 vanilla pod • 250g (9oz) double cream
For the passion fruit jelly: 6 leaves of gelatine • 600ml (1 pint) passion fruit juice
Equipment: 8–10 × 10cm (4in) tartlet tins • baking beans, dried pulses, or raw rice

1. To make the shortcrust pastry, knead the butter, icing sugar, and egg in the bowl of a mixer fitted with a dough hook. Add the almonds and flour and work swiftly to a smooth consistency. Shape into a ball, press flat, wrap in cling film and refrigerate for at least 2 hours.

2. Preheat the oven to 180°C (350°F/Gas 4) and butter the tins. Divide the pastry into 8 to 10 pieces. Roll out each piece on a lightly floured work surface or between 2 pieces of cling film to a 5mm (¼in) thick disc around 12cm (5in) in diameter. Use these to line the tins. Trim off any overhanging pastry and prick all over with a fork.

3. Line the pastry with baking parchment and fill with baking beans. Blind-bake on the middle shelf of the oven for around 10 minutes. Remove the baking beans and parchment and return the pastry cases to the oven for 5–10 minutes until golden brown. Remove and leave to cool in the tins.

4. Meanwhile, stir together the eggs with the sugar and blancmange mix in a bowl with the balloon whisk. Soak the gelatine in cold water for 10 minutes. Put the milk in a saucepan with the passion fruit purée, butter, and vanilla seeds and bring to the boil, stirring constantly. Have an empty bowl ready next to the hob.

5. Pour the boiling milk mixture over the egg mixture, stirring constantly. Return this to the saucepan and cook for around 1 minute over a medium heat, stirring constantly with the balloon whisk, before decanting into the previously prepared empty bowl. Squeeze out the gelatine and stir into the hot mixture until it has dissolved. Let the mixture cool until it is lukewarm. Whip the cream until it is just holding its shape, then fold it in.

6. Finely chop the white chocolate and melt it in a heatproof bowl over simmering water (don't let the bowl touch the water). Brush the tartlet bases with white chocolate and leave to set. Fill each tart with the still-lukewarm cream filling to around 5mm (¼in) below the rim of the pastry case, smooth out the cream, and leave to cool.

7. To make the passion fruit jelly, soak the gelatine in cold water for 10 minutes. Heat one-third of the passion fruit juice in a saucepan. Squeeze out the gelatine and dissolve it in the warmed juice, then stir in the remaining juice. Pour the jelly over the cooled tartlets so it comes up to the rim and leave for 2 hours in the refrigerator until the jelly has set.

▼

STRAWBERRY AND RASPBERRY TART

with a vanilla crumble base

For the crumble base: **50g (1¾oz) unsalted butter, chopped • 100g (3½oz) rye flour • 40g (1¼oz) light brown sugar • 1 tsp vanilla powder**
For the strawberry and raspberry ganache: **350g (12oz) white chocolate • 125g (4½oz) unsalted butter • 75g (2½oz) strawberry purée (with 10% sugar, see p219) • 75g (2½oz) raspberry purée (with 10% sugar, see p219) • 100g (3½oz) caster sugar • 20g (¾oz) liquid glucose (see p219)**
For decoration: **Mascarpone Cream (see p104) • strawberries and raspberries • lemon verbena leaves (see p168)**
Equipment: **2 × 12cm (5in) cake rings • piping bag with round nozzle**

Makes 2   Prep: 40 mins + 2 hrs chilling + cooling   Baking time: 10–15 mins

Chocolate-based tarts are all too often rather heavy. In this recipe, the chocolate is balanced by the acidity of raspberries and strawberries and the hearty crunch of the crumble base. Mascarpone cream and lemon verbena play their part, too, in moderating the richness of the ganache.

1. Preheat the oven to 190°C (375°F/Gas 5). Place the cake rings alongside each other on a baking tray lined with baking parchment.

2. To make the crumble, mix the butter, flour, sugar, and vanilla powder, and work swiftly to a crumble consistency, either by rubbing with your fingertips or using a mixer fitted with a dough hook. For a more regular crumble you could push the mixture through a coarse sieve. Divide the crumble between the cake rings and press down gently. Bake on the middle shelf of the preheated oven for 10–15 minutes. Remove from the oven and leave to cool.

3. To make the ganache, chop the white chocolate and the butter. Gently heat the fruit purées with the sugar and glucose, pour over the chopped chocolate and stir well. Finally, beat in the butter with a hand-held blender, taking care not to incorporate any air.

4. Pour the ganache over the vanilla crumble and chill in the refrigerator for around 2 hours. Put the mascarpone cream into a piping bag fitted with a round nozzle and decorate the tart with some blobs of cream. Arrange berries between the blobs of cream, and garnish with lemon verbena leaves.

▼

CHERRIES

from the Black Forest

Makes 12   Prep: 50 mins + 3 hrs freezing + cooling   Baking time: 8 mins

For the sponge: **50g (1¾oz) dark chocolate** • **40g (1¼oz) unsalted butter** • **5 eggs** • **40g (1¼oz) plain flour** • **40g (1¼oz) cocoa powder** • **140g (5oz) good-quality marzipan** • **45g (1½oz) icing sugar** • **45g (1½oz) caster sugar**
For the mascarpone cream: **5 leaves of gelatine** • **375g (13oz) double cream** • **750g (1lb 10oz) mascarpone** • **75g (2½oz) caster sugar** • **75ml (2½fl oz) kirsch** • **100g (3½oz) cherries, pitted**
For the glazed cherries and decoration: **20g (¾oz) vanilla blancmange mix** • **200ml (7fl oz) cherry juice** • **50g (1¾oz) caster sugar** • **seeds from 1 vanilla pod** • **1 cinnamon stick** • **250g (9oz) cherries** • **milk chocolate shavings**
For the cherry jam: **10g (¼oz) granulated sugar** • **1g (¼ tsp) agar agar** • **125g (4½oz) cherries** • **50g (1¾oz) jam sugar** • **juice of 1 lemon** • **seeds from ½ vanilla pod**
Equipment: **6cm (2½in) round cutter (optional)** • **2 × 6-hole silicone hemisphere baking moulds (each hole 6cm / 2½in)**

1. Preheat the oven to 180°C (350°F/Gas 4) and line a baking tray with baking parchment. Chop the chocolate. Melt the butter with the chocolate in a saucepan over a low heat. Separate 4 eggs. Whisk the egg yolks with the remaining whole egg and put the egg whites into a separate bowl. Combine the flour and cocoa powder.

2. Beat the marzipan and icing sugar together in a bowl using an electric hand whisk. Gradually mix in the egg yolk mixture, taking care to ensure that you don't get any lumps. Whisk the egg whites in a bowl using the scrupulously cleaned electric hand whisk on a medium setting until they are just holding their shape, gradually trickling in the caster sugar as you do so. Carefully fold around half the whipped egg whites into the marzipan and egg mixture, then fold in the flour mixture and the remaining egg whites. Finally, fold in the melted butter and chocolate.

3. Spread the sponge mixture out on the baking parchment until it is 1–1.5cm (½–¾in) high. Bake on the middle shelf of the preheated oven for 7–8 minutes, taking care that the sponge doesn't dry out too much. Remove from the oven and leave to cool in the tray. Then turn the sponge out of the tray, remove the baking parchment and use a cutter or glass to stamp out 12 × 6cm (2½in) circles.

4. Soak the gelatine for the mascarpone cream in cold water for 10 minutes. Whip the cream in a bowl using an electric hand whisk until it is just holding its shape. Stir the mascarpone together with the sugar in a bowl. Heat the kirsch in a pan, squeeze out the gelatine and dissolve it in the warmed liquid. Stir 2–3 tbsp of the mascarpone mixture into the kirsch mixture, then swiftly combine this with the remaining mascarpone cream. Fold the cream into the mascarpone. Fill the silicone moulds with the mixture, then press 2–3 cherries into each and top with a stamped-out sponge circle. Put into the freezer for around 3 hours.

5. To decorate, stir the vanilla blancmange mix with 3–4 tbsp cherry juice until smooth. Bring the remaining cherry juice to the boil in a saucepan with the sugar, vanilla seeds, and cinnamon, stir in the vanilla blancmange mixture to thicken the juice mixture. Remove the cinnamon stick, stir in the cherries and leave to cool until it is lukewarm. To make the jam, combine the granulated sugar with the agar agar. Bring to the boil in a saucepan with the remaining ingredients, remove from the heat, and leave to cool. Mix it up again and press through a sieve. Decorate the little cakes with blobs of cherry jam, glazed cherries, and milk chocolate shavings.

▼

BLUEBERRY TART

with lavender and honey

For the crumble base and decoration: 125g (4½oz) unsalted butter, at room temperature, plus extra for the tins • 115g (4oz) plain flour, plus extra for the tins • 100g (3½oz) light brown sugar • 25g (scant 1oz) honey • 125g (4½oz) ground almonds • ½ tsp ground lavender petals • blueberries • white chocolate decorations (see p218)
For the blueberry cream: 190g (6½oz) dark chocolate (66% cocoa solids) • 215g (7½oz) double cream • 40g (1¼oz) liquid glucose (see p219) • 190g (6½oz) blueberry purée (with 10% sugar; see p219) • 2 tsp blueberry liqueur
For the blueberry jelly (optional): 1 sachet of clear cake glaze (from mail order companies) • 100g (3½oz) blueberry purée (with 10% sugar; see p219) • 50g (1¾oz) blackberry purée (with 10% sugar; see p219)
Equipment: 6 × 12cm (5in) tartlet tins

Makes 6   Prep: 30 mins + cooling   Baking time: 10–15 mins

1. Preheat the oven to 190°C (375°F/Gas 5). Butter the tartlet tins and dust with flour, knocking out any excess flour.

2. To make the crumble, mix the butter and sugar in a bowl. Add the honey, flour, almonds, and lavender and work everything swiftly together to form a crumble, using your fingertips or a mixer fitted with a dough hook. To create a more regular crumble you could push the mixture through a coarse sieve. Spread over the base of the tins and press down gently, spreading some of the mixture up the sides. Bake the bases on the middle shelf of the preheated oven for 10–15 minutes until golden brown. Remove from the oven and leave to cool in the tins.

3. Meanwhile, chop the chocolate for the blueberry cream into little pieces and melt in a heatproof bowl over simmering water (don't let the bowl touch the water). Put 110g (4oz) of the cream into a saucepan with the glucose and bring to the boil. Remove from the hob and stir in the blueberry purée and liqueur.

4. Combine the hot blueberry mixture with the chocolate using a spatula until you have a smooth, shiny mixture. Add the remaining cream and mix it using a hand-held blender. Take care when doing this to incorporate as little air as possible. Spread the cream filling evenly and smoothly over the tartlet bases and leave to cool.

5. If desired, prepare the cake glaze for the jelly topping, following the packet instructions. Stir in the blueberry and blackberry purées to combine thoroughly with the glaze. Leave to cool briefly, then spread over the tartlets.

6. Dip the blueberries in the jelly and set them on top of the tartlets. If you like, use a spoon to add little drops of the jelly on top and decorate with white chocolate decorations. Keep cold until ready to serve.

Tip: decorate the tarts
I like to "airbrush" these little tarts. To do this, put the tartlets in the freezer for at least 2 hours. Melt 200g (7oz) cocoa butter over simmering water and stir with 400g (14oz) white couverture chocolate until melted. Transfer this into an airbrush gun and spray onto the tartlets. You won't need all the mixture, but the airbrush gun needs to be filled with a certain quantity to work properly.

▼

APPLE AND PEAR TART

with almonds and acacia honey cream

For the pastry: 135g (4¾oz) unsalted butter, chopped, plus extra for the tin • 85g (3oz) icing sugar • 1 egg • 1 tsp vanilla powder • pinch of salt • seeds from ¼ vanilla pod • 225g (8oz) plain flour, plus extra for the tin and for dusting • 30g (1oz) ground almonds
For the caramelized almonds: 50g (1¾oz) blanched almonds • 1 tbsp icing sugar
For the topping: 150g (5½oz) icing sugar • 75g (2½oz) ground almonds • 150g (5½oz) unsalted butter, at room temperature • 3 eggs • 1½ tbsp vanilla blancmange mix • 60g (2oz) acacia honey • seeds from ½ vanilla pod • pinch of salt • 1 tart, firm apple • 1 pear
For the Chantilly cream: 200g (7oz) double cream • 50g (1¾oz) caster sugar • seeds from 1 vanilla pod
Equipment: 24cm (9½in) tart tin • baking beans, dried pulses, or raw rice

Serves 8   Prep: 50 mins + 2 hrs chilling + cooling   Baking time: 35–45 mins

1. To make the shortcrust pastry, knead the butter with the icing sugar, egg, vanilla powder, salt, and vanilla seeds in the bowl of a mixer fitted with a dough hook. Add the flour and almonds and work everything swiftly to a smooth consistency. Shape the pastry into a ball, press flat, wrap in cling film, and refrigerate for at least 2 hours.

2. For the caramelized almonds, preheat the oven to 190°C (375°F/Gas 5). Roast the almonds on a baking tray on the middle shelf of the preheated oven for around 8 minutes. Add them to a frying pan, sprinkle with the icing sugar, and let them caramelize evenly over a medium heat, stirring constantly. Leave to cool on a baking tray and set aside. Do not turn off the oven.

3. Butter the tart tin and dust with flour, knocking out any excess. Roll out the pastry on a lightly floured work surface or between 2 pieces of cling film to a 5mm (¼in) thick circle and use this to line the tin. Trim off any overhanging pastry and prick all over with a fork.

4. To blind-bake the pastry, line it with baking parchment and fill with baking beans to weigh it down. Cook on the middle shelf of the preheated oven for around 12 minutes. Take it out of the oven

and remove the baking beans and parchment. Let the pastry case cool in the tin. Reduce the oven temperature to 180°C (350°F/Gas 4).

5. Meanwhile, make the topping by mixing together the icing sugar, almonds, butter, eggs, vanilla blancmange, honey, vanilla seeds, and salt in a bowl using an electric hand whisk and beating until you have a smooth creamy consistency. When you are doing this try to incorporate as little air as possible. Peel, halve, and core the apple and pear. Cut the fruit into slices roughly 5mm (¼in) thick.

6. Put the cream mixture into the pastry case and alternately arrange the apple and pear slices on top. Finish baking the tart on the middle shelf of the oven for 25–30 minutes. Remove it from the oven and leave to cool in the tin.

7. To make the Chantilly cream, whip the double cream with the sugar and vanilla seeds.

8. Put the caramelized almonds into a freezer bag and crush them with a rolling pin. Carefully release the cooled tart from the tin and decorate with quenelles of Chantilly cream and the almond pieces.

▼

MERINGUE TARTLETS

with strawberries

Makes 15
Prep: 50 mins + 2½ hrs chilling + cooling   Baking time: 15 mins

For the pastry: 135g (4¾oz) unsalted butter, chopped • 80g (2¾oz) icing sugar • 1 egg • 1 tsp vanilla powder • pinch of salt • seeds from ½ vanilla pod • 225g (8oz) plain flour, plus extra for dusting • 30g (1oz) ground almonds
For the filling: 5 egg yolks • 1 sachet of vanilla blancmange mix • 250ml (9fl oz) milk • 250g (9fl oz) double cream • seeds from 1 vanilla pod • 75g (2½oz) caster sugar
For the meringue and decorations: 50g (1¾oz) white chocolate • 750g (1lb 10oz) strawberries • 3 egg whites • pinch of salt • 140g (5oz) caster sugar • finely grated zest of ½ lime • milk chocolate decorations (see p218)
Equipment: 15-hole silicone tartlet baking mould (each hole 4.5cm / 1½in diameter), or other tartlet tins of that size • baking beans, dried pulses, or raw rice • piping bag with small round nozzle

1. To make the shortcrust pastry, knead the butter, icing sugar, egg, vanilla powder, salt, and vanilla seeds in the bowl of a mixer fitted with a dough hook. Add the flour and almonds and work swiftly until smooth. Shape into a ball, press flat, wrap in cling film, and refrigerate for at least 2 hours.

2. To make the filling, stir together the egg yolks and blancmange mix in a bowl with a balloon whisk. Put the milk in a saucepan with the cream, vanilla seeds, and sugar, and bring to the boil. Gradually add this to the egg yolk mixture, stirring constantly. Return the mixture to the pan and briefly return to the boil to thicken, stirring all the time. Push through a sieve into a bowl, cover with cling film and leave to cool in the refrigerator.

3. Preheat the oven to 190°C (375°F/Gas 5). Roll out the shortcrust pastry on a lightly floured work surface or between 2 sheets of cling film until it is around 3mm (⅛in) thick. Then stamp out 15 × 5.5cm (2¼in) circles using a cutter or a glass. Line the silicone moulds with the pastry circles. Trim off any overhanging pastry and prick all over with a fork. Line each pastry case with baking parchment and weigh it down with some baking beans. Bake on the middle shelf of the preheated oven for around 12 minutes until golden brown. Take out of the oven and remove the baking beans and parchment. Leave to cool in the tins.

4. Chop the white chocolate into little pieces and melt it in a heatproof bowl over simmering water (don't let the bowl touch the water). Brush the pastry cases with the chocolate and leave to set. Carefully release the pastry cases from the tins and put them on a baking tray.

5. Stir the vanilla blancmange again with the balloon whisk until it is smooth, transfer it to a piping bag fitted with a small round nozzle and pipe it into the pastry cases in large blobs. Halve the strawberries and lay them out in a circular pattern on top. Chill the tartlets for around 30 minutes in the refrigerator.

6. Preheat the oven to 220°C (425°F/Gas 7), if possible just have the upper heating element in the oven turned on. Whisk the egg whites in a bowl using an electric hand whisk on a medium setting until they are stiff, gradually adding the salt and sugar as you go. Fold in the lime zest. Transfer the meringue to a piping bag fitted with a small round nozzle and pipe onto the tartlets. Bake on the upper shelf of the oven for around 2 minutes until light brown, taking care that it doesn't get too dark. Leave to cool on a wire rack. Use to decorate the tartlets, adding the milk chocolate decorations.

▼

CHOCOLATE MARSHMALLOW TREATS

with hidden raspberries

For the waffle bases: 40g (1¼oz) unsalted butter • 40g (1¼oz) caster sugar • 1 tsp vanilla powder • pinch of salt
• 1 egg • 80ml (2¾fl oz) milk • 80g (2¾oz) plain flour • flavourless vegetable oil, if necessary
For the marshmallow filling and raspberries: 8 leaves of gelatine • 65g (2¼oz) egg whites (from 2–3 eggs)
• 50g (1¾oz) caster sugar • 75g (2½oz) liquid glucose • 2 tsp raspberry vinegar • about 250g (9oz) raspberries
For the icing: 500g (1lb 2oz) dark chocolate • 80ml (2¾fl oz) flavourless vegetable oil, or cocoa butter
Equipment: thin waffle maker (ice cream cone maker) • 5cm (2in) round cutter (optional)
• sugar thermometer or kitchen thermometer • piping bag with medium round nozzle

Makes 20–25   Prep: 40 mins + 1 hr chilling + cooling   Baking time: 1 hr

1. To make the waffles, melt the butter in a saucepan over a low heat. Stir together the butter, sugar, vanilla powder, and salt in a bowl. Mix in the egg and the milk. Sift over the flour and mix this in too.

2. Heat the waffle maker and, if necessary, lightly brush with oil. Bake thin waffles from the mixture, using around 3 tbsp for each. Immediately each waffle is cooked, stamp out 5cm (2in) circles using a cutter or a glass. Preheat the oven to 70°C (160°F/Gas ¼). Lay the waffle discs onto a baking tray and let them dry out on the middle shelf of the oven for around 30 minutes. Remove from the oven and leave to cool.

3. To make the marshmallow filling, soak the gelatine in cold water for 10 minutes. Put the egg whites into a food processor fitted with a whisk attachment and beat on a medium setting until they are just holding their shape. Switch the machine to a slower setting and let it continue running. Heat the sugar with the glucose and 100ml (3½fl oz) of water in a pan until it reaches 113°C (235°F), checking the temperature using a thermometer. As soon as the correct temperature is reached, switch the food processor back to a medium setting, pour the sugar syrup slowly into the whipped egg whites and beat for 1 minute. Squeeze out the gelatine and stir it into the mixture. Continue to beat until the mixture has cooled to room temperature, adding the raspberry vinegar as you whisk.

4. Put a few raspberries on each of the biscuits. Transfer the marshmallow mixture to a piping bag fitted with a medium round nozzle and pipe this on top. Cover and refrigerate for around 1 hour to allow the marshmallow mixture to firm up.

5. To make the icing, finely chop the chocolate and melt it in a heatproof bowl over simmering water (don't let the bowl touch the water). Stir in the oil, incorporating as little air as possible. If necessary, let the icing cool down a bit, it should be no more than 40°C (104°F). Cover the marshmallow treats with the icing to seal completely, and keep chilled until ready to serve.

Tip: chocolatey biscuit
You could also try coating the
biscuit bases with some melted
chocolate to prevent them from
becoming soft.

▼

MINI HAZELNUT CAKES

with cranberry mousse

For the sponge: **6 eggs** • **70g (2¼oz) milk chocolate** • **50g (1¾oz) unsalted butter**
• **75g (2½oz) good-quality marzipan** • **115g (4oz) caster sugar** • **pinch of salt** • **40g (1¼oz) plain flour**
• **40g (1¼oz) ground hazelnuts, plus extra for sprinkling**
For the mousse: **5 leaves of gelatine** • **250g (9oz) double cream** • **4–5 egg whites** • **90g (3¼oz) caster sugar**
• **3 egg yolks** • **80g (2¾oz) cranberries** • **305g (10oz) cranberry jam**
For the chocolate pastry: **90g (3¼oz) unsalted butter, chopped** • **55g (2oz) icing sugar** • **1 egg** • **pinch of salt**
• **150g (5½oz) plain flour, plus extra for dusting** • **20g (¾oz) cocoa powder**
For the chocolate icing and decoration: **375g (13oz) dark chocolate** • **375g (13oz) almond brittle**
• **225g (8oz) double cream** • **225ml (7½fl oz) milk** • **ready-made poured fondant or glacé icing (see p219)**
Equipment: **2 × 6-hole silicone hemisphere baking moulds (each hole 6cm / 2½in diameter)**

Makes 12   Prep: 50 mins + 4½ hrs chilling + cooling   Baking time: 15–20 mins

Cranberries are often misjudged on account of their bitter flavour, but they really come into their own
in baking. Here they are softened by hazelnut, creating a scintillating taste experience.

1. Preheat the oven to 200°C (400°F/Gas 6). Line
a baking tray with baking parchment. Separate 4 of
the eggs. Stir the egg yolks with the 2 whole eggs.
Chop the milk chocolate finely and let it melt in a
heatproof bowl over simmering water (don't let the
bowl touch the water). Melt the butter and stir it
into the chocolate.

2. Beat the marzipan and 50g (1¾oz) of the sugar in
a bowl using an electric hand whisk. Gradually stir
in the egg yolk mixture, taking care that you don't
get any lumps. Beat the egg whites with the salt in
a bowl using an electric hand whisk on a medium
setting until they are stiff, gradually adding the
remaining sugar as you go. Fold the whipped egg
whites into the marzipan mixture. Combine the
flour and hazelnuts and fold these in too. Finally,
fold in the melted chocolate mixture.

3. Spread the mixture evenly over the baking
parchment. It should be about 1cm (½in) thick. Use
a sieve to evenly distribute ground hazelnuts over
the mixture to cover. Bake on the middle shelf of
the preheated oven for 6–9 minutes, taking care that
it doesn't dry out too much.

4. Remove the sponge from the oven and let it
cool in the tray. Then turn it out onto a second piece
of baking parchment and remove the upper sheet
of parchment. Use a cutter or glass to stamp out
12 × 6cm (2½in) cake bases.

5. To make the cranberry mousse, soak the gelatine
in cold water for 10 minutes. Whip the cream until
it is stiff. Then beat the egg whites until they, too,
are stiff, trickling in 40g (1¼oz) of the sugar as you
do. Beat the egg yolks in a heatproof bowl with the

remaining sugar over simmering water until they reach a ribbon consistency. Squeeze out the gelatine and stir it into the egg yolk mixture. Gradually fold in the egg whites, alternating with the cream. Finally, fold in the cranberries and jam.

6. Transfer the mousse into the silicone moulds and top each one with a cake base. Put the little cakes into the freezer for at least 4 hours.

7. Meanwhile, preheat the oven to 180°C (350°F/ Gas 4). Knead together all the ingredients for the pastry in a mixer fitted with a dough hook until smooth. Wrap in cling film and chill for 30 minutes. Roll it out thinly on a lightly floured work surface or between 2 sheets of cling film and stamp out 12 × 6cm (2½in) bases using a cutter or glass. Bake in the hot oven for 8–9 minutes.

8. To make the icing, chop the chocolate and brittle into little pieces. Bring the cream and milk to the boil in a saucepan. Add the chocolate and brittle, remove from the heat, and mix everything thoroughly using a hand-held blender. Take care not to incorporate any air. Let it cool slightly.

9. Brush the pastry bases with a little of the chocolate icing. Release the frozen cakes from the moulds and place them on the pastry bases. Then decorate with the remaining chocolate icing and blobs of lukewarm glacé or poured fondant icing.

▼

CHOCOLATE LAYER CAKE

with cranberries

Serves 12   Prep: 50 mins + 4 hrs chilling + cooling   Baking time: 20–25 mins

For the sponge: 75g (2½oz) unsalted butter • 50g (1¾oz) dark chocolate, chopped • 150g (5½oz) plain flour
• 1 tsp baking powder • 60g (2oz) cocoa powder • 6 eggs • pinch of salt • 175g (6oz) caster sugar
For the mousse: 5 leaves of gelatine • 250g (9oz) double cream • 4–5 egg whites • 90g (3¼oz) caster sugar
• 3 egg yolks • 600g (1lb 5oz) cranberry jam
For the icing and decoration: 80g (2¾oz) milk chocolate • 80g (2¾oz) dark chocolate • 80g (2¾oz) nougat
• 4½ tbsp milk • 50g (1¾oz) double cream • good-quality ready-rolled marzipan • cocoa nibs • cocoa powder
Equipment: 26cm (10in) springform tin or cake ring

1. Preheat the oven to 180°C (350°F/Gas 4) and line the base of the tin with baking parchment. Melt the butter and chocolate in a saucepan over a low heat. Combine the flour, baking powder, and cocoa.

2. Separate the eggs. Beat the egg whites with the salt in a bowl using an electric hand whisk on a medium setting until they are stiff, gradually adding 125g (4½oz) of the sugar as you go. Beat the egg yolks with the remaining sugar in a second bowl until creamy. Put the whipped egg white mixture on top of the creamy egg yolks, sift over the flour mixture, then gradually fold everything together. Finally, fold in the melted butter and chocolate.

3. Spoon the batter into the tin and bake on the middle shelf of the hot oven for 20–25 minutes. Remove from the oven and leave to cool in the tin. Release from the tin, remove the baking parchment and slice twice horizontally to get 3 layers.

4. For the mousse, soak the gelatine in cold water for 10 minutes. Whip the cream until stiff. Then beat the egg whites until stiff, gradually adding 40g (1¼oz) of the sugar. Beat the yolks and remaining sugar over simmering water until they reach a ribbon consistency. Squeeze out the gelatine and stir into the egg yolk mix. Gradually fold in the egg whites alternating with the cream, then half the jam.

5. Lay the bottom sponge layer in the springform tin or cake ring and spread with a thin layer of cranberry jam. Cover with one-third of the mousse, smoothing it out over the cake. Lay the middle sponge layer on top and likewise spread with jam and one-third of the mousse. Place the final sponge layer on top and cover with the remaining mousse. Cover and put into the freezer for at least 4 hours.

6. To make the chocolate icing, chop both types of chocolate and the nougat finely. Bring the milk and cream to the boil in a saucepan, stir in the chocolate and let it melt. Beat in the nougat with a hand-held blender, taking care not to incorporate any air. Leave to cool slightly.

7. Place a wire rack on a baking tray or piece of baking parchment. Release the cake from the ring, cover with the ready-rolled marzipan, place it on the wire rack and cover the sides with the warm icing. Put the cake in the refrigerator until the icing has set. Scatter the sides of the cake with cocoa nibs and dust the centre with cocoa powder.

▼

CHAMPAGNE CREAM DIAMONDS

Classy yet understated

For the filling: 180ml (6fl oz) champagne • 1½ tbsp lemon juice • 125g (4½oz) caster sugar • 2 egg yolks • 40g (1¼oz) vanilla blancmange mix • 250g (9oz) unsalted butter, at room temperature
For the sponge: 175g (6oz) good-quality marzipan • 5 egg yolks • 4 egg whites • 40g (1¼oz) unsalted butter • 40g (1¼oz) dark chocolate (67% cocoa solid) • 40g (1¼oz) plain flour • 20g (¾oz) cocoa powder • 50g (1¾oz) caster sugar
For the icing and decoration: 375g (13oz) dark chocolate couverture • 375g (13oz) almond brittle • 225g (8oz) double cream • 225ml (7½fl oz) milk • high-quality single-origin chocolate (if desired, by mail order from pâtisserie suppliers) • 50g (1¾oz) white chocolate couverture (optional)
Equipment: 12-hole silicone diamond mould, or 12-hole silicone hemisphere mould

Makes 15   Prep: 1 hr + 32 hrs chilling + cooling   Baking time: 20 mins

1. One day in advance, prepare the champagne cream filling by bringing 125ml (4fl oz) of the champagne to the boil in a saucepan with the lemon juice and sugar. Meanwhile, stir together the remaining champagne, egg yolks, and blancmange mix in a bowl with a balloon whisk. Gradually pour the boiling champagne mixture into the egg yolk mixture, stirring constantly. Return the mixture to the saucepan and cook for around 1 more minute to thicken, stirring all the time. Transfer into a bowl, cover the surface with cling film and leave to cool, then chill in the refrigerator for 24 hours.

2. The following day, preheat the oven to 190°C (375°F/Gas 5) and line a baking tray with baking parchment ready to make the sponge. Use an electric hand whisk to beat the marzipan and 1 egg yolk together in a bowl until smooth. Gradually mix in the remaining egg yolks until you have a smooth consistency. Add 3½ tbsp of water and 1 egg white and beat everything until it is creamy.

3. Chop the butter and chocolate finely. Melt both in a heatproof bowl over simmering water (don't let the bowl touch the water). Sift the flour with the cocoa powder. Beat the remaining egg whites with an electric hand whisk on a medium setting until stiff, gradually adding the sugar as you go. Stir the chocolate mixture into the marzipan mixture. Then gradually alternately fold in the flour mixture and the whipped egg whites.

4. Spread the sponge mixture out evenly over the baking tray and bake on the middle shelf of the preheated oven for around 20 minutes. Remove from the oven and leave to cool on the tray. Use a round cutter or glass to stamp out 15 × 6cm (2½in) circles.

5. Cream the butter for the filling in a bowl using an electric hand whisk until it is pale and fluffy. Gradually beat in the cooled champagne cream. Fill the moulds with the cream and seal each off with a sponge disc. Freeze for around 6 hours.

6. To make the icing, finely chop the dark chocolate couverture and brittle. Bring the cream and milk to the boil in a saucepan. Add the chocolate and brittle and combine thoroughly using a hand-held blender. When doing this, take care not to incorporate any air. Let the icing cool down until warm.

7. Line a baking tray with baking parchment and set a wire rack on top. Release the diamonds from their moulds and put them on the wire rack. Cover with the icing. If you like, blend the high-quality single-origin chocolate to a powder in a food processor and use this to sprinkle around the lower rims of the diamonds. Put into the refrigerator.

8. To make the chocolate decorations, melt the white chocolate couverture as before and spread it out thinly on baking parchment. Lay another sheet of baking parchment on top and roll it out thinly again with a rolling pin. Keep this chocolate sheet in the refrigerator until ready for use. To serve, break it into pieces and use these to decorate the diamonds.

▼

PUFF PASTRY

For the puff pastry (basic pastry or détrempe):
40g (1¼oz) unsalted butter • 1 tsp salt
• 250g (9oz) plain flour
For the puff pastry (beurrage):
160g (5¾oz) unsalted butter • 50g (1¾oz) plain flour,
plus extra for dusting

1. One day in advance, prepare the puff pastry
(basic pastry or détrempe) by melting the butter in a
saucepan over a low heat. Stir the salt into 125ml (4fl
oz) of water in a bowl. Add the flour and melted butter
and knead to a smooth consistency. Wrap in cling film
and leave to rest in the refrigerator for 24 hours.

2. The following day, chop the butter for the
beurrage into pieces, put it into a bowl with the flour
and use a mixer fitted with a dough hook to knead
to a smooth consistency. Shape into a rectangular
slab, wrap in cling film and refrigerate for around
30 minutes.

3. To finish preparing the puff pastry, roll out the
beurrage to form a 20cm (8in) square. Roll out the
pastry on a lightly floured work surface to form a
40 × 22cm (16 × 8½in) rectangle. Place the beurrage
centrally on the pastry and fold over the edges so the
beurrage slab is completely enveloped. Wrap the whole
thing in cling film and refrigerate for 30 minutes.

4. Roll out the puff pastry and complete a single
fold: roll out the pastry to form a 40 × 20cm
(16 × 8in) rectangle and remove excess flour. Fold
one-third of the pastry up over the middle third of
the pastry, then fold the final third down so you
have 3 layers of pastry lying on top of each other.

5. The next step is to perform a double fold: roll
out the pastry once more to a 40 × 20cm (16 × 8in)
rectangle. Now work from the 2 short edges: fold in

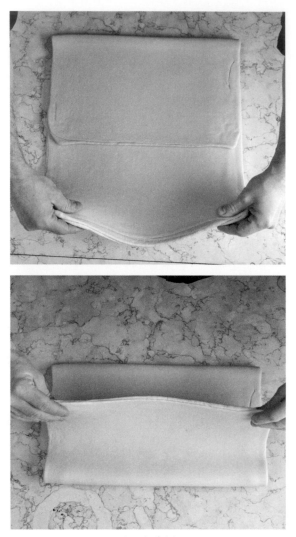

Single fold

one-quarter of the pastry on both sides towards the
centre so that the 2 short edges meet in the middle
of the pastry sheet. Then fold the pastry over once
again along the centre line, to produce 4 layers.
Wrap in cling film and return to the refrigerator
to chill for 1 hour.

6. Repeat the single and then double folds so that in
total you perform 2 single folds and 2 double folds.
Return the pastry to the refrigerator again for at least
1 hour before use.

▼

CROISSANT DOUGH

For the dough (basic yeasted dough or détrempe):
500g (1lb 2oz) plain flour • ½ tsp salt • 200ml (7fl oz)
milk • 70g (2¼oz) caster sugar • 30g (1oz) fresh yeast
• 1 egg • 30g (1oz) unsalted butter, at room temperature
For the croissant dough (beurrage):
400g (14oz) unsalted butter • 120g (4¼oz) plain flour

1. To make the croissant dough (basic yeasted dough
or détrempe), combine the flour and salt in a large
bowl. Heat the milk until it is lukewarm. Mix the sugar
and the crumbled yeast with the milk and stir until the
yeast dissolves. Add the milk mixture, egg, and butter
to the flour and knead everything for 10 minutes until
you have a dough with a smooth elastic consistency. If
necessary knead in a bit more flour or milk.

2. On a large floured board, shape the dough into
a ball and cut the surface centrally with a knife in a
cross shape to extend around halfway down through
the dough. Cover with a clean tea towel and leave to
prove for 30 minutes at room temperature.

3. Meanwhile, chop the butter for the beurrage into
pieces and knead these together with the flour in the
bowl of a mixer fitted with a dough hook. Shape
into a rectangular slab, wrap in cling film and
refrigerate for around 30 minutes.

4. Roll out the beurrage to a 20cm (8in) square. Roll
out the risen dough in all 4 directions from the middle
to form an evenly thick 40 × 22cm (16 × 8½in)
rectangle and remove any excess flour. Lay the
beurrage slab centrally on the yeasted dough sheet and
fold the edges of the dough over so that the butter is
completely enveloped. Take care when doing this that
the butter and the dough are roughly equally firm and
that the dough above and below the butter is equally
thick. The dough should have no openings or cracks
through which the fat could escape during rolling.

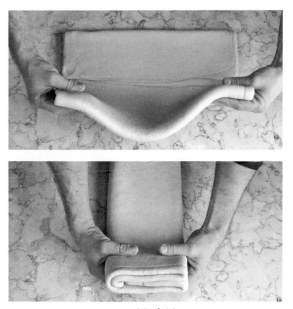

Double fold

5. Rolling out the dough. The first thing to do is
to complete a single fold: carefully roll out the dough
to form a 40 × 20cm (16 × 8in) rectangle. Fold
one-third of the dough up over the central third
of the dough and then fold the final third down over
this so that you end up with 3 overlapping layers of
dough. Roll out the dough again to form an even
40 × 20cm (16 × 8in) rectangle. Wrap the dough
securely in cling film and chill in the refrigerator
for at least 20 minutes.

6. The next step is to perform a double fold: working
from the 2 short edges of the sheet, fold in one-
quarter of the dough from each side towards the
centre so that the 2 short edges meet in the middle
of the sheet. Then fold the dough over once again
along the centre line so that you get 4 layers of dough
lying on top of each other. Roll it out again to form a
40 × 20cm (16 × 8in) rectangle, wrap securely in
cling film, and chill in the refrigerator for at least
another 20 minutes.

7. Repeat the single and then double fold so that you
perform a total of 2 single folds and 2 double folds.

▼

TEMPERED CHOCOLATE DECORATIONS

300g (10oz) chocolate (as specified in the recipe)
Equipment: sugar thermometer or kitchen thermometer
• marble slab

1. Roughly chop the chocolate. Melt two-thirds of it over simmering water and heat to 45–50°C (113–122°F). Take care that no water gets into it.

2. Remove from the heat and slowly sprinkle in the remaining chocolate, stirring, until it has melted, and the mixture has cooled to 31–32°C (88–90°F). If it cools too much, reheat it briefly over the simmering water until it reaches 32°C (90°F) once more.

3. Spread the tempered chocolate in a thin layer over the marble slab with a spatula. Leave the chocolate to set for at least 2 hours in a cool, dry place, then cut into the desired shape and lift from the slab. If you don't immediately need the entire quantity, save the rest for your next baking session.

▼

SOURCES

Sous Chef
15 Tottenham Lane
London
N8 9DJ
www.souschef.co.uk

SLR Supplies Ltd
Unit 3, The Orbital Centre
Southend Road
IG8 8HD
www.slrsupplies.com

ACKNOWLEDGEMENTS

Special thanks are owed to Oliver Edelmann and Frank Nagel, my mentors.
For all their support on the photo shoots we would like to thank:

The team: Jan C. Brettschneider and Christian Hümbs (in front), Fabian Fiedler, Niko Langner and Janina Alff (behind)

▼

BAKING NOTES

Sponge leftovers   Any sponge left over after cutting out cake bases can be whizzed in a food processor fitted with a cutting blade and used instead of flour to sprinkle inside cake tins, or even as a sweet enhancement to your breakfast muesli. Larger sponge pieces are also ideal for making a trifle-style dessert: just layer them up with some Mascarpone Cream (see p104) and serve in glass bowls, so the attractive layers are visible.

Fruit purées   In my recipes I use only the fruit purées made by the company Boiron (available by mail order). They have a sugar content of 10%. If you use other purées, or if you try to produce your own purées from fresh or frozen fruit, the quality of your baking may suffer, as the products from Boiron are made using a specific process to reduce the water content in the fruits, which makes an enormous difference to the end result.

Use fruit powders   Since macarons are extremely sensitive to moisture (even high humidity levels in the weather or your kitchen can have an impact on their consistency), I try to use as little liquid as possible in all the ganache recipes. For this reason, I like to use fruit powders, which give a good fruity flavour but with the liquid component completely removed. These can be obtained easily from mail order companies for speciality and pâtisserie products (see left).

Gelatine   Mixing the dissolved gelatine with cold ingredients must be done very swiftly, stirring constantly so that no lumps of gelatine can form. To be safe, it is usually best to first stir 1–2 tbsp of the cold mixture into the dissolved gelatine to equalize the temperature.

Liquid glucose   In the recipes in this book which contain chocolate or cream, I usually use liquid glucose instead of sugar. Liquid glucose is a concentrated juice obtained from starch. In contrast to granulated sugar, it is better at bonding the water present in both of these ingredients (chocolate and cream). It's also good to know that it is not as sweet as regular household sugar.

Shortcrust pastry   Freshly made shortcrust pastry is usually too soft to be rolled out, it would have to be pressed into the tin by hand and you can never get it completely smooth that way. So to produce flat and even tart bases I first put the pastry in the refrigerator for a few hours until it is a bit firmer, but still supple enough to be rolled out. If the pastry is chilled for too long, it loses that suppleness and simply crumbles when you try to roll it out.

Oven temperature   Unless otherwise specified, the oven temperatures relate to the upper and lower heating elements in a standard non-convection oven. For a fan oven, the temperature should be reduced by around 20°C (68°F). You should also refer to the oven manufacturer's guidelines if necessary.

Glacé icing / poured fondant   Ready-made glacé icing can be found in the baking section at the supermarket; the poured fondant which professional chefs prefer is best obtained from mail order suppliers of speciality and pâtisserie products (see left). But the ingredients for a quick and simple glacé icing can be found in virtually everyone's store cupboard, so there's no need to rush to the shops: mix 100g (3½oz) icing sugar with around 2 tsp of water, lemon juice or dark rum until you have a spreadable consistency... and you're done!

▼ INDEX

A

Advocaat Cupcakes 27
almonds
    Amaretti 55
    Apple and Pear Tart 205
    Apricot Cake 77
    Blueberry Cake 158
    Blueberry Tart 202
    Cantuccini 56
    Chocolate Tarts 59
    Cookie Sandwich 45
    Crunchy Nougat 51
    Financiers 102
    German Cheesecake 84
    Honeyed Cupcakes 147
    Macarons see Macarons
    Milanese Cherry Tartlets 119
    Nut Wedges 133
    Poppy Seed Tart 154
    Profiteroles 123
    Red Wine Cake 62
    Soured Cream Tarts 60
    Swedish Almond Cake 137
    Swiss Nut Tartlets 135
    Viennese Apple Strudel 124
Amaretti 55
American Cheesecake 80
apples
    Apple and Pear Tart 205
    Fruited Rye Loaf 127
    Hazelnut and Apple Cookies 40
    Peanut Butter Apple Muffins 18
    Tarte Tatin 115
    Viennese Apple Strudel 124
    Yeasted Apple Cake 150–51
apricots
    Apricot Cake 168
    Apricot Cake with Almonds 77
    Fruited Rye Loaf 127
    Sachertorte 130–31

B

bananas
    Banana Cupcakes 22
    Coconut Banana Muffins 16
    Exotic Muffins 143
    Walnut Cookies 39
basic principles of baking 9–10
beetroot: White Chocolate Muffins 30
berries
    Cronuts with Berries 90
    Millefeuille Pastries 193
    see also individual berries
blackberries
    Cronuts with Blackberries 90
    Millefeuille Pastries 193
    Red Berry Compote Cupcakes 145
blackcurrants
    Cassis Macarons 177
    Millefeuille Pastries 193
blueberries
    Blueberry Cake 158
    Blueberry Macarons 186
    Blueberry Madeira Cake 69
    Blueberry Tart 202
    Millefeuille Pastries 193
    Red Berry Compote Cupcakes 145
    Soured Cream Tarts 60
brownies
    Green Tea Brownies 152
    Peanut Butter Brownies 98
buckwheat flour 158
    Apricot Cake 168
    Blueberry Cake 158

C

cakes
    Apricot Cake 77
    Apricot Cake with Buckwheat 168
    Blueberry Cake 158
    Blueberry Madeira Cake 69
    Carrot Cake 93
    Chocolate Bundt Cake 66
    Chocolate Layer Cake 213
    Dresden Sugar Cake 75

Dutch Cream Cake 138–39
    Lime Pound Cake 70
    Marble Cake 65
    Millefeuille Cake 163
    Orange Cake 116
    Red Wine Cake 62
    Rhubarb Cake 72
    Sachertorte 130–31
    Swedish Almond Cake 137
    Yeasted Apple Cake 150–51
    see also small cakes
Cantuccini 56
caramel
    Advocaat Cupcakes 27
    Apple and Pear Tart 205
    Caramel Macarons 181
    Coffee Cheesecake 83
    Cronuts with Praline Cream 190–191
    Macadamia Caramel Cookies 43
    Peanut Butter Apple Muffins 18
    Peanut Butter Brownies 98
    Pecan Slices 149
    Walnut and Red Wine Muffins 29
carrots
    Carrot Cake 93
    Carrot and Mascarpone Cupcakes 189
Cassis Macarons 177
Champagne Cream Diamonds 214–15
cheesecakes
    American Cheesecake 80
    Cheesecake Muffins 86
    Coffee Cheesecake 83
    German Cheesecake 84
Chelsea Buns 110
cherries
    Cherries From the Black Forest 201
    Cherry-Chocolate Tartlets 164
    Dutch Cream Cake 138–39
    Milanese Cherry Tartlets 119
    Red Berry Compote Cupcakes 145
    Rice Pudding Muffins 32
    Spelt and Cherry Muffins 21

chocolate 10
  Carrot and Mascarpone Cupcakes 189
  Champagne Cream Diamonds 214–15
  Cheesecake Muffins 86
  Cherries From the Black Forest 201
  Cherry-Chocolate Tartlets 164
  Chocolate Bundt Cake 66
  Chocolate Chip Cookies 36
  Chocolate Layer Cake 213
  Chocolate Marshmallow Treats 208
  Chocolate Tarts 59
  Coconut Ginger Macaroons 52
  Cookie Sandwich 45
  Crunchy Nougat 51
  Dutch Cream Cake 138–39
  Éclairs with Chocolate Orange Cream 107
  Green Tea Brownies 152
  Home-made Marshmallows 95
  Macarons with Chocolate or Nougat Filling 172–73
  Marble Cake 65
  Meringue Tartlets 207
  Milanese Cherry Tartlets 119
  Milk Slices 35
  Mini Hazelnut Cakes 210–11
  Molten Chocolate Cakes 46
  Nut Wedges 133
  Passion Fruit Tartlets 197
  Peanut Butter Brownies 98
  Pecan Slices 149
  Piedmont Hazelnut Tart 112–13
  Raspberry Hedgehogs 167
  Red Berry Compote Cupcakes 145
  Sachertorte 130–31
  Strawberry and Raspberry Tart 198
  Swedish Almond Cake 137
  Swiss Nut Tartlets 135
  tempered chocolate decorations 219
  White Chocolate Muffins 30
  Yuzu Tart 161

choux pastry
  Éclairs with Chocolate Orange Cream 107
  Éclairs with Strawberries 104–05
  Profiteroles 123
coconut
  Coconut Banana Muffins 16
  Coconut Ginger Macaroons 52
  Mango and Coconut Muffins 16
coffee
  Coffee Cheesecake 83
  Tiramisu 120
cookies
  Chocolate Chip Cookies 36
  Cookie Sandwich 45
  Hazelnut and Apple Cookies 40
  Linz Biscuits 129
  Macadamia Caramel Cookies 43
  Walnut Cookies 39
cranberries
  Chocolate Layer Cake 213
  Mini Hazelnut Cakes 210–11
  Swiss Nut Tartlets 135
cream cheese
  American Cheesecake 80
  Cheesecake Muffins 86
  Coffee Cheesecake 83
  German Cheesecake 84
creams
  advocaat cream 27
  blueberry cream 202
  buttercream 135
  champagne cream 214
  Chantilly cream 62, 112, 205
  cheesecake cream 86
  chocolate orange cream 107
  crème brûlée 194
  crème pâtissière 110, 150, 158
  lemon verbena cream 187
  mascarpone cream 93, 104, 119, 120, 123, 189, 198, 201
  praline cream 22, 190
  vanilla cream 147, 157, 193
Crème Brûlée Tart 194
croissant dough 217
cronuts
  Cronuts with Berries 90

  Cronuts with Praline Cream 190–91
  Cronuts with Yuzu Jelly 157
cupcakes
  Advocaat Cupcakes 27
  Banana Cupcakes 22
  Carrot and Mascarpone Cupcakes 189
  Honeyed Cupcakes 147
  Raspberry Cupcakes 15
  Red Berry Compote Cupcakes 145
  Strawberry Cupcakes 24

D
Doughnuts 89
Dresden Sugar Cake 75
Dutch Cream Cake 138–39

E
éclairs
  Éclairs with Chocolate Orange Cream 107
  Éclairs with Strawberries 104–05

F
figs
  Fruited Rye Loaf 127
  Tarte Tatin 115
Financiers 102
fondant, poured 219
fruit powders 219
fruit purées 219
Fruited Rye Loaf 127

G
ganache
  Baileys ganache 112
  blueberry and sesame ganache 186
  caramel ganache 181
  cassis ganache 177
  chocolate ganache 172
  lychee and green tea 182
  matcha and passion fruit ganache 180
  nougat ganache 172
  raspberry ganache 176

strawberry and raspberry ganache 198

white chocolate ganache 24, 145, 161, 167

gelatine 219

German Cheesecake 84

ginger
  Coconut Ginger Macaroons 52
  Lime Pound Cake 70

glacé icing 219

green tea
  Green Tea Brownies 152
  Lychee Macarons 182
  Matcha Macarons 180
  Yuzu Tart 161

H

hazelnuts
  Chelsea Buns 110
  Cherry-Chocolate Tartlets 164
  Chocolate Chip Cookies 36
  Cronuts with Praline Cream 190–91
  Fruited Rye Loaf 127
  Hazelnut and Apple Cookies 40
  Linz Biscuits 129
  Mini Hazelnut Cakes 210–11
  Nut Wedges 133
  Piedmont Hazelnut Tart 112–13
  Swiss Nut Tartlets 135
  Yeasted Apple Cake 150–51

honey
  Apple and Pear Tart 205
  Blueberry Tart 202
  Honeyed Cupcakes 147
  Spelt and Cherry Muffins 21

L

Lemon Madeleines 101

Lemon Verbena Macarons 187

limes
  Exotic Muffins 143
  Lime Pound Cake 70

Linz Biscuits 129

liquid glucose 219

Lychee Macarons 182

M

macadamia nuts
  Green Tea Brownies 152
  Macadamia Caramel Cookies 43

macarons 172–87
  basic recipe 172–73
  Blueberry Macarons 186
  Caramel Macarons 181
  Cassis Macarons 177
  Lemon Verbena Macarons 187
  Lychee Macarons 182
  Macarons with Chocolate or Nougat Filling 172–73
  Matcha Macarons 180
  Raspberry Macarons 176

Macaroons, Coconut Ginger 52

Madeleines 101

mangoes
  Exotic Muffins 143
  Mango and Coconut Muffins 16

maple syrup
  Nut Wedges 133
  Pecan Slices 149
  Swiss Nut Tartlets 135

Marble Cake 65

marshmallows
  Chocolate Marshmallow Treats 208
  Chocolate Marshmallows 95
  Strawberry Marshmallows 96

marzipan
  Blueberry Madeira Cake 69
  Champagne Cream Diamonds 214–15
  Cherries From the Black Forest 201
  Chocolate Layer Cake 213
  Mini Hazelnut Cakes 210–11
  Piedmont Hazelnut Tart 112–13
  Sachertorte 130–31

Matcha Macarons 180

meringue
  Meringue Tartlets 207
  Rhubarb Cake 72

Milanese Cherry Tartlets 119

Milk Slices 35

Millefeuille Cake 163

Millefeuille Pastries 193

Molten Chocolate Cakes 46

muesli: Blueberry Madeira Cake 69

muffins
  Cheesecake Muffins 86
  Coconut Banana Muffins 16
  Exotic Muffins 143
  Peanut Butter Apple Muffins 18
  Rice Pudding Muffins 32
  Spelt and Cherry Muffins 21
  Walnut and Red Wine Muffins 29
  White Chocolate Muffins 30

N

nougat
  Banana Cupcakes 22
  Chocolate Layer Cake 213
  Crunchy Nougat 51
  Macarons with Chocolate or Nougat Filling 172–73
  Piedmont Hazelnut Tart 112–13
  Profiteroles 123
  Raspberry Hedgehogs 167

Nut Wedges 133

O

oats
  Banana Cupcakes 22
  Blueberry Madeira Cake 69
  Hazelnut and Apple Cookies 40

oranges
  Éclairs with Chocolate Orange Cream 107
  Orange Cake 116

oven temperatures 219

P

passion fruit
  American Cheesecake 80
  Exotic Muffins 143
  Matcha Macarons 180
  Passion Fruit Tartlets 197

pastries
  Éclairs with Chocolate Orange Cream 107
  Éclairs with Strawberries 104–05
  Millefeuille Pastries 193
  Prifiteroles 123
  Viennese Apple Strudel 124

see also tarts
peanuts
Nut Wedges 133
Peanut Butter Apple Muffins 18
Peanut Butter Brownies 98
pears
Apple and Pear Tart 205
Poppy Seed Tart 154
pecans
Nut Wedges 133
Pecan Slices 149
Piedmont Hazelnut Tart 112–13
polenta: Orange Cake 116
Poppy Seed Tart 154
Profiteroles 123
puff pastry
basic recipe 216
Cronuts 157, 190–91
Dutch Cream Cake 138–39
Millefeuille Cake 163
Millefeuille Pastries 193
Tarte Tatin 115

R
raspberries
Chocolate Marshmallow Treats 208
Linz Biscuits 129
Millefeuille Pastries 193
Raspberry Cupcakes 15
Raspberry Hedgehogs 167
Raspberry Macarons 176
Red Berry Compote Cupcakes 145
Strawberry and Raspberry Tart 198
Red Berry Compote Cupcakes 145
Red Wine Cake 62
redcurrants: Red Berry Compote Cupcakes 145
Rhubarb Cake 72
Rice Pudding Muffins 32
Rum Babas 108

S
Sachertorte 130–31
sauces
caramel sauce 43

chocolate sauce 145
shortcrust pastry 219
Apple and Pear Tart 205
Chocolate Tarts 59
Crème Brûlée Tart 194
Dutch Cream Cake 138–39
Meringue Tartlets 207
Millefeuille Cake 163
Nut Wedges 133
Passion Fruit Tartlets 197
Poppy Seed Tart 154
Soured Cream Tarts 60
Swiss Nut Tartlets 135
small cakes
Champagne Cream Diamonds 214–15
Cherries From the Black Forest 201
Financiers 102
Madeleines 101
Mini Hazelnut Cakes 210–11
Molten Chocolate Cakes 46
soured cream
American Cheesecake 80
Apricot Cake 168
Coffee Cheesecake 83
Soured Cream Tarts 60
Spelt and Cherry Muffins 21
sponge leftovers 219
strawberries
Dutch Cream Cake 138–39
Éclairs with Strawberries 104–05
Meringue Tartlets 207
Millefeuille Pastries 193
Strawberry Cupcakes 24
Strawberry Marshmallows 96
Strawberry and Raspberry Tart 198
Sugar Cake, Dresden 75
Swedish Almond Cake 137
Swiss Nut Tartlets 135

T
Tarte Tatin 115
tarts
Apple and Pear Tart 205
Blueberry Tart 202
Cherry-Chocolate Tartlets 164

Chocolate Tarts 59
Crème Brûlée Tart 194
Meringue Tartlets 207
Milanese Cherry Tartlets 119
Passion Fruit Tartlets 197
Piedmont Hazelnut Tart 112–13
Poppy Seed Tart 154
Soured Cream Tarts 60
Strawberry and Raspberry Tart 198
Swiss Nut Tartlets 135
Tarte Tatin 115
Yuzu Tart 161
Tiramisu 120

V W
Viennese Apple Strudel 124
waffles
Chocolate Marshmallow Treats 208
Waffles, Belgian 48
walnuts
Carrot Cake 93
Carrot and Mascarpone Cupcakes 189
Chocolate Chip Cookies 36
Fruited Rye Loaf 127
Walnut Cookies 39
Walnut and Red Wine Muffins 29
White Chocolate Muffins 30

Y
yeast dough
Chelsea Buns 110
croissant dough 217
Cronuts with Berries 90
Cronuts with Praline Cream 190–91
Cronuts with Yuzu Jelly 17
Doughnuts 89
Dresden Sugar Cake 75
Rum Babas 108
Yeasted Apple Cake 150–51
yuzu 10
Cronuts with Yuzu Jelly 157
Yuzu Tart 161

Christian Hümbs is a skilled chef and pâtissier. The places he has worked read like a "Who's Who" of the stars of gastronomy: Johann Lafer's Stromburg, the Louis C. Jacob on the Elbchaussee in Hamburg, La Mer on the island of Sylt, or the Aqua in Wolfsburg, one of the world's finest restaurants and – with 3 stars – the most highly rated in Germany. Now he is employed at the 2-star restaurant Haerlin at the Fairmont Hotel Vier Jahreszeiten, where he is responsible for what is currently considered by connoisseurs to be "the most exciting finale in the republic". Hümbs's creations are characterized by their sophistication and unusual combinations, but he values simple and classic desserts and cakes just as highly. He became known to the general public as a judge on the German TV show "The Big Bake". In 2014 he was awarded the title Pâtissier of the Year.

Jan C. Brettschneider has been photographing food for publishers, magazines, and advertisers for more than 20 years. During his countless photographic trips and studio jobs he has collaborated with many top chefs, wine makers, and producers, both nationally and internationally. His passion for fine food and drink paired with his instinct for lighting and style produces pictures which truly whet your appetite and which have won him many awards. Jan C. Brettschneider lives with his family in Hamburg.

 Penguin Random House

Recipes Christian Hümbs
Text Julia Bauer
Photography Jan C. Brettschneider
Food styling Christian Hümbsr
Editing Karin Kerber, Julia Bauer
Design, typography, implementation
Sibylle Schug, Astrid Shemilt

For DK Germany
Publisher Monika Schlitzer
Editorial management Caren Hummel
Project support Sarah Weiß
Production management Dorothee Whittaker
Production Inga Reinke
Production coordination Katharina Dürmeier

For DK UK
Translator Alison Tunley
Editor Lucy Bannell
Project editor Kathryn Meeker
Senior art editor Glenda Fisher
Jacket designer Amy Keast
Managing editor Stephanie Farrow
Managing art editor Christine Keilty
Creative technical support Sonia Charbonnier
Senior pre-producer Tony Phipps
Senior producer Stephanie McConnell

First published in Great Britain in 2016 by
Dorling Kindersley Limited
80 Strand, London, WC2R 0RL

Copyright © 2016 Dorling Kindersley Limited
A Penguin Random House Company
10 9 8 7 6 5 4 3 2 1
001–289744–Jul/2016

A CIP catalogue record for this book
is available from the British Library.
ISBN: 978-0-2412-4225-4

Printed and bound in China

All images © Dorling Kindersley Limited
For further information see: www.dkimages.com

A WORLD OF IDEAS:
SEE ALL THERE IS TO KNOW

www.dk.com